ON POETS
AND
OTHERS

TITLES BY OCTAVIO PAZ AVAILABLE FROM
ARCADE PUBLISHING

Alternating Current
Conjunctions and Disjunctions
Marcel Duchamp: Appearance Stripped Bare
The Monkey Grammarian
On Poets and Others

Octavio Paz

On Poets
and
Others

TRANSLATED FROM THE SPANISH BY
MICHAEL SCHMIDT

ARCADE PUBLISHING • NEW YORK

First Arcade edition 1990
First Skyhorse Publishing edition 2014

Some of the material in this volume has appeared previously in the following
publications: *In/Mediaciones*, 1979; *Plural* 30, March 1974; *Plural* 51, December
1975; *El País*, 1980; *Alternating Current*, 1967; *Sur*, July 1943; *El Arcoyla Cira*,
1956; *Poetry Nation*, 1975.

Arcade Publishing books may be purchased in bulk at special discounts for
sales promotion, corporate gifts, fund-raising, or educational purposes. Special
editions can also be created to specifications. For details, contact the Special Sales
Department, Arcade Publishing, 307 West 36th Street, 11th Floor, New York,
NY 10018 or arcade@skyhorsepublishing.com.

Arcade Publishing® is a registered trademark of Skyhorse Publishing, Inc.®, a
Delaware corporation.

Visit our website at www.arcadepub.com.

10 9 8 7 6 5 4 3 2 1

Library of Congress Cataloging-in-Publication Data is available on file.

Cover design by Owen Corrigan

ISBN: 978-1-62872-374-8
Ebook ISBN 978-1-62872-392-2

Printed in the United States of America

CONTENTS

CONTENTS

FOREWORD

When you meet Octavio Paz, you have the impression you're meeting *all* of him. He seems to contain all his ages. There is about him, and about the way he moves and laughs, often at himself, something of the adolescent. Here is the student striding through the streets of Mexico City at night arguing politics, discussing Dostoevski, with his schoolmates, joining the student strike in 1929. Here, too is the young idealist who went to the Yucatan in his early twenties to help found a school for the children of the sisal workers; and then went to Spain during the Civil War. Paz is recognizably the young disciple of the surrealist André Breton; and he retains the charismatic luster of controversial diplomat and teacher. Paz doesn't repudiate his past, and, unlike Nietzsche—whom he admires, and who systematically refused to revise his early work because, as he put it, "the young man he had been would have despised the older man he had become"—Paz is often willing to revise work he wrote four decades ago. It may be that poems are never finished, only abandoned—but still, Paz returns to some of them, drawing them a little farther along the road.

In many of the essays contained in this collection, Paz describes the relations of this young man—himself—with his elder and more established writers and philosophers. Robert Frost, Luis Cernuda, José Ortega y Gasset, William Carlos Williams, Ezra Pound, André Breton, all appear here to have been influences in Paz's life. In each of them he finds something to build on. And if ultimately he rejects them all, it is ruefully, an almost filial estrangement. Octavio Paz is a "pluralist." One of his favorite critical terms is *pluralism* in culture. Paz is deeply rooted in the cultures of the Spanish language. The poets and philosophers of France and England marked him, as did the various cultures and overwhelming erotic art of India. In each he finds ways of understanding his own culture. They show him different routes back to the beginning. French lucidity, even in revolution; English continuity, despite changes of the world outside; Indian mysticism, especially the mysticism of the body—all these help Paz home, to himself and his own culture, overlaid as it is by patterns of violence and repression.

Writing at the time of Breton's death, Paz notes: "All of us who had anything to do with Breton experienced a dual, dizzying feeling: fascination and a centrifugal impulse. I confess that for a long time I was kept awake by the worry that I might do or say something to provoke his reproof. I believe many of his friends had a similar experience. . . . I should say that I write as if I were engaged in a silent dialogue with Breton: reply, answer, coincidence, disagreement, homage, all together. Even as I write this I experience that feeling." Under Breton's influence, Paz tried automatic writing and produced his great prose-poems. But it's interesting that in his valedictory essay on Breton, Paz quotes none of his master's poetry, only his critical statements. The English critic Jason Wilson suggests that Breton was an influence on Paz's poetics more than on the poetry itself, and I suspect he's right. In Paz there is a double impulse: first, an enthusiasm for ideas, especially ideas about poetry and poetic traditions. He is brilliant at recounting the history of artistic trends of this and last century, the modernist "tradition of discontinuity" called up in the titles of books such as *Conjunctions and Disjunctions* and *Alternating Current*. But at the other pole of his imaginative thought, T. S. Eliot has left a deep mark on his work. Eliot is in almost every way the opposite of Breton. Paz rejects Eliot's religion and politics; but he can't resist the actual poems and the literary essays.

Like other radical writers before him, Paz locates the intellectual poverty of much of Latin America in the fact that the eighteenth century—the great critical century, the Enlightenment—passed it by. While the United States was colonized by the spirit of the Reformation, Latin America suffered the Counter-Reformation. Without an Enlightenment, the critical disciplines that developed in France and England were not practiced in the Spanish colonies. Paz provides some benefits of the Enlightenment for Latin America. He is not alone in this, and he doesn't set out to write like Voltaire. But he produces social and literary criticism—for him the two are inseparable—which he has set in the French tradition of "moralism."

His most famous prose book is *The Labyrinth of Solitude*, published in 1950 and revised in 1959. In it he explores the Mexican psyche and tries to place Mexican history back within the Mexican himself. As he put it in an interview a decade ago, he wanted to "recover the consciousness" of a country that history had pushed aside. "One of the pivotal ideas of the book," he said, "is that there is a Mexico which is buried but alive. Or, more accurately, there is in Mexican men and women a universe of buried images, desires and impulses. I attempted a description—inadequate of course, little more than a glimpse—of the world of repressions, inhibitions, memories, appetites and dreams which Mexico has been and is." *The Labyrinth of Solitude* has fascinated two intellectual generations in Latin America. It is one of those rare keys to a culture that usually seems to be written by critics from the outside. Paz's rare achievement was to write as an insider, with passion *and* detachment. He has said, "Already at that time I thought as I do now, that history is a form of knowledge set between science properly speaking and poetry. Historical knowledge is not quantitative nor can the historian discover historical laws. The historian describes things like a scientist and has visions like a poet." His "history" is not in chronological sequence. Paz brings facts and images to the foreground and holds them still while he examines them minutely, tracing their origins, discovering their latencies. There are elements of autobiography in the images chosen. When Paz writes about the rituals for the day of the dead, the little offerings of sugar, clay, and raffia are peculiarly vivid. He grew up near where these things were made and as a child strayed among the craftsmen's workshops. The relations between such images and the beliefs they reveal are teased out, now lovingly, now angrily. When Paz distinguishes firmly between ideas and beliefs, he follows his philosophical teacher José Ortega y Gasset. Ideas are changeable, in movement; beliefs are largely static and constant. "A man is defined more by what he believes than by what he thinks," Paz says. Paz *partly* believes, and in this he is typical of many modern writers. There is a withholding which is painful because the writer remains at the crossroads, his journey forever incomplete.

Skepticism and openness make it possible for Paz to see his world and his history freshly. Since the wars of independence, Latin Americans have tended to despise the earlier colonial periods. Paz emphasizes the decades of relative plenty and stability and the great cultural achievement of the colony. He underlines the political balances of power that existed between church and state. His aim isn't to apologize for the colonial system, but to restore a balance in our perception, to counter the automatic rhetoric that prevails in teaching and writing. Until the colonial period is integrated into the memory of Latin Americans, an essential part of the past remains repressed.

In *The Labyrinth of Solitude* Paz makes another unpopular point. He insists on the place of the brutal Emiliano Zapata in the Mexican Revolution, but he assigns to him an unexpected destiny. Zapata's project was an "attempt to return to origins." According to Paz, "the paradox of Zapatismo was that it was a profoundly traditionalist movement; and precisely in that traditionalism its revolutionary might resides. To put it more clearly, because it was traditionalist, Zapatismo was radically subversive." Zapata becomes for Paz a political talisman for his own poetic quest of *return*. Zapata's movement "signifies revelation, the emergence of certain hidden and repressed realities. It is revolution not as ideology but as an instinctive movement, an explosion which is the revelation of a reality prior to hierarchies, classes, property." I think the phrase "revolution not as ideology" is the key to his political writing.

In 1936, the Chilean poet Pablo Neruda arranged for Octavio Paz to go to Spain at the time of the Civil War. In Spain Paz did not like what he saw of the machinations of the Popular Front and its patrons. He began to question his kind of Marxist allegiances. His doubts were heightened by the Nazi-Soviet pact and later by his estrangement from Neruda. Ideological politics became for him the great seduction and the great tragedy of the writers of this and the last century. "The history of modern literature, from the German and English romantics to our own days, is the history of a long, unhappy passion for politics. From Coleridge to Mayakovski, Revolution has been the great Goddess, the eternal beloved and the great whore to poets and novelists. Politics filled Malraux's head with smoke, poisoned the sleepless nights of Cesar Vallejo, killed García Lorca, abandoned the old poet Antonio Machado in a village in the Pyrenees, locked Pound in an asylum, dishonoured Neruda and Aragon, has made Sartre a figure of ridicule, and has acknowledged Breton all too late. But we can't disown politics; it would be worse than spitting at the sky, spitting at ourselves." In one of his finest poems, the "Nocturne of San Ildefonso," he writes:

> The good, we sought the good:
>   to straighten out the world.
> We did not lack integrity:
>   we lacked humility.
> What we wanted we wanted without innocence.

His bitterness is hardly surprising. While Paz is a highly respected and loved poet, he remains a figure of controversy, and that controversy is political. The Latin American intellectual world is largely committed to the left in rather old-fashioned ways. And Paz represents another kind of radicalism. He began to define it when he published an article in the Argentinean magazine *Sur*, edited by Victoria Ocampo. She was the only editor brave enough to print it back in 1951. The article was on the Soviet labor camps. Paz had been collecting information about them with growing horror. If socialism was to claim any moral authority, it would have urgently to come to terms with the aberrations of Stalinism. When the piece appeared, Paz anticipated debate. Instead, it was greeted with public silence and with private abuse. Neruda was prominent among his accusers. He was "giving ammunition to the enemy"—namely the United States. Better suppress the truth, common sense said. Paz writes in the same poem,

> Poetry,
>   the bridge suspended between history and truth,
> is not a way towards this or that:
>   it is to see
> the stillness within movement.

In those lines he says something with which few of his fellow Latin American poets would agree. He refuses to put his art to use.

He remains a radical, but a radical who rejects ideologies. Paz sees his task in these terms: "The writer should be a sniper, he should endure solitude, he should know himself to be a marginal being. It is both a curse and a blessing that we writers are marginal." He also says: "Criticism is the apprenticeship of the revising imagination—imagination cured of fantasy and resolved to confront the world's reality. Criticism tells us that we ought to learn to dissolve the idols, learn to dissolve them in ourselves. We have to learn to be air, dream set free." This is no recipe for passivity. Paz has learned his own lesson. "Criticism reveals the possibility of liberty and this is an invitation to action." The failure of democracy in Latin America is a failure of criticism. Technological progress without a critical capacity gives us "more things, not more being."

Criticism is a discipline that keeps language to its meanings. "When a society becomes corrupt," he writes, "what first grows gangrenous is language. Social criticism, therefore, begins with grammar and the reestablishment of meanings." Even so, the true writer has an uneasy relationship with his language. For Paz the natural metaphor is an erotic one: "I believe the writer's attitude to language should be that of a lover: fidelity and, at the same time, a lack of respect for the beloved object. Veneration and transgression."

Opposite this caring and necessarily violent lover, he identifies the enemy—the enemy both of the individual and of the collective: the bureaucratic state perverted by ideology. This state he defines as *The Philanthropic Ogre* in one of his books of political essays: a cold, totalitarian monster that devours its children without appetite, mechanically, chewing hard.

Octavio Paz came up hard against that ogre at the end of his diplomatic career. From 1962 to 1968 he was Mexican ambassador to India. In 1968, the Olympic Games were staged in Mexico City, and radical students assembled huge demonstrations. One of them ended in a massacre—no one is quite sure how many people were killed. This outrage revealed to Paz what he had long suspected—the inability of the Mexican system to respond to democratic pressure. The written constitution remained a luminous fiction, the rhetoric of politics grew increasingly remote from the huge, hungry, unemployed sub-proletariat that had swamped the major cities. He could no longer represent the Mexican government. His resignation had considerable political effect. He spoke later of the "vitiated intellectual atmosphere" of Mexico. "Among us," he declared, "ideological simplifications dominate and our intellectuals do not show much respect for reality."

When he returned to Mexico two years later, he was a painful thorn in the side of the political establishment. But increasingly he also became an irritant to radical intellectuals. After his resignation he had been vested with great authority. Now he rejected the popular accolade and preferred to continue on his own way. His critical essays have not made comfortable reading for anyone. During the last ten years he has alienated many people in my generation and in the one before. They tend to see Paz as someone who has taken the conventional journey from left to right. They say his early work exceeds his later work in scope and quality. But for younger writers he is once again clearly a teacher and guide. He makes himself available, he encourages their work, he is a genuine solitary radical, a man in search of roots, and he responds to evidence of that search in others.

To be sure, the best early poems are major; but it is in the more recent collections and long poems, where he traces his way back through his culture, that he accomplishes what he set out to do over half a century ago. He carries less cultural luggage now—memory has done its sifting and what remains is the essential, the unforgettable, the things of which he is himself made.

When he stepped away from political in-fighting and stood alone, he found his great subject not only in his Mexico's past but in his own. His life has spanned years of critical change in Latin America. He has seen the ends of a dozen dreams and his beloved cities dehumanized by overcrowding, pollution, destitution, almost as tragically as the cities of India. It is the end not only of dreams but of cultures and communities; in such places, how can the dream be set free?

Through his father and grandfather, Paz has the next best thing to a firsthand memory of nineteenth-century Mexico, when liberalism triumphed for a time. During this time the tensions which distort present-day Mexico did not exist. His most recent magazine is *Vuelta*, one of the most influential journals in Latin America. He is a wonderfully imaginative editor, one who invites into the Mexican arena an incongruous and stimulating range of intelligences from Europe and the rest of his own continent. For him, no subject is taboo. The title of the magazine implies turn, return, or turning back. His last major collection of poems, published in 1974, is also entitled *Vuelta*. In Emiliano Zapata, André Breton, and the writers and artists he admires, and in the religious and erotic traditions he explored during his years in India, he is looking for origins, sources, and the fresh resources that flow from them.

He spent his childhood in the village of Mixcoac, a suburb of Mexico City. It has an Aztec name and some broken walls survive from pre-conquest times. If you scratch about in your garden there you sometimes find potsherds. There are also colonial buildings—nothing very striking, but solid and permanent. There are examples of later architecture, too, and an inner ring road that reminds you that this is 1986 and nothing is safe against the ravages of technology. Nothing except memory and the sensitive eye registering its place in this visual anthology of popular Mexican history. Octavio Paz's grandfather, Ireneo, dominated the house where he grew up. Ireneo was a lawyer and a liberal reformer who fought against the French and wrote more than ten books. He edited a daily paper for thirty-eight years. To Paz the child, he was an old and disheartened man. He had fallen in, probably reluctantly, behind the strong man—the dictator Porfirio Díaz—and his cause was defeated by the revolution. Octavio Paz's father rebelled against Ireneo. Liberalism had failed. He supported something more radical, the revolution, and especially the agrarian reform which Zapata stood for. He was an agent and then a propagandist for Zapata. When the poet was a boy, old Zapatistas used to visit, bringing delicious, strange foods from their pueblos. They made a marked impression on the boy: they seemed to contain the turbulent history he was too young to remember. Paz's father, who became an alcoholic, died tragically in a train crash in 1935.

> My father went and came back through the flames.
>
> Among the sleepers and the rails
>   of a station swarming with flies and dust
> One afternoon we gathered up his pieces.
>   I was never able to speak with him.
> I find him now in dreams.
> That half-erased country of the dead.

The poet's mother was a Mexican of Spanish background. She was not cultured, but she was affectionate and supportive. He speaks of her tenderly as "a love letter with errors in the grammar."

In my opinion, his finest poem is "Pasado en Claro" which means "Fair Draft" or, as a translator has it, "A Draft of Shadows"; it was published in 1975. The energy of the language and the imaginative penetration of this poem set it in a class by itself. It evokes the long history of ritual, repression, and change in Mexico, but also Paz's own life, which in this context becomes ours as much as Wordsworth's does in *The Prelude*. He declares a debt to Wordsworth not only in the way the poem works but in the epigraph:

> Fair seed-time had my soul, and I grew up
> Foster'd alike by beauty and by fear.

Beauty and fear. In a sense, they are the twin poles not only of Paz's life but also of his work.

—MICHAEL SCHMIDT

ON POETS
AND
OTHERS

ROBERT FROST:
VISIT TO A POET

After twenty minutes walking along the highway under a three
o'clock sun, I came at last to the turning. I veered right and began
to climb the slope. At intervals, the trees along the path provided
a little coolness. Water ran down a small brook, through the
undergrowth. The sand squeaked under my tread. Sun was everywhere. In the air there was a scent of green, hot growth, thirsty.
Not a tree, not a leaf stirred. A few clouds rested heavily, an-
chored in a blue, waveless gulf. A bird sang. I hesitated: "How
much nicer it would be to stretch out under this elm! The sound
of water is worth more than all the poets' words." I walked on
for another ten minutes. When I got to the farm, some fair-haired
children were playing around a birch tree. I asked for the master;
without interrupting their game, they replied, "He's up there, in
the cabin." And they pointed to the very summit of the hill. I set

1

off again. Now I was walking through deep undergrowth that came up to my knee. When I reached the top I could see the whole little valley; the blue mountains, the stream, the luminously green flatland, and, at the very bottom, the forest. The wind began to blow; everything swayed, almost cheerfully. All the leaves sang. I went toward the cabin. It was a little wooden shack, old, the paint flaked, grayed by the years. The windows were curtainless; I made a way through the underbrush and looked in. Inside, sitting in an easy chair, was an old man. Resting beside him was a woolly dog. When he saw me the man stood up and beckoned me to come around the other side. I did so and found him waiting for me at the door of his cabin. The dog jumped up to greet me. We crossed a little passage and went into a small room: unpolished floor, two chairs, a blue easy chair, another reddish one, a desk with a few books on it, a little table with papers and letters. On the walls three or four engravings, nothing remarkable. We sat down.

"Sure is hot. You want a beer?"

"Yes, I believe I do. I've walked half an hour and I'm worn out."

We drank the beer slowly. While I sipped mine, I took him in. With his white shirt open—is there anything cleaner than a clean white shirt?—his eyes blue, innocent, ironic, his philosopher's head and his farmer's hands, he looked like an ancient sage, the kind who prefers to observe the world from his retreat. But there was nothing ascetic in his looks, rather a manly sobriety. There he was, in his cabin, removed from the world, not to renounce it but to see it better. He wasn't a hermit nor was his hill a rock in the desert. The three crows hadn't brought him the bread he ate; he'd bought it himself in the village store.

"It's really a beautiful place. It almost seems real. This landscape is very different from ours in Mexico, it's made for men to look at. The distances are made for our legs, too."

2

"My daughter's told me the landscape of your country's very dramatic."

"Nature is hostile down there. What's more, we're few and weak. Man is consumed by the landscape and there's always the danger you might turn into a cactus."

"They tell me that men sit still for hours there just doing nothing."

"Afternoons you see them, completely still, by the roadsides or at the entrances to towns."

"Is that how they do their thinking?"

"It's a country that's going to turn to stone one day. The trees and the plants all tend to stone, just as the men do. And the animals, too: dogs, coyotes, snakes. There are little baked clay birds and it's very strange to see them fly and hear them sing, because you never get used to the idea they're real birds."

"When I was fifteen I wrote a poem. My first poem. And you know what it was about? *La noche triste*. I was reading Prescott then, and maybe reading him set me thinking about your country. Have you read Prescott?"

"That was one of my grandfather's favorite books, so I read him when I was a boy. I'd like to read him again."

"I like rereading books, too. I don't trust folk who don't reread. And those who read a lot of books. It seems crazy to me, this modern madness, and it'll only increase the number of pedants. You've got to read a few books well and frequently."

"A friend tells me they've invented a way of developing speed-reading. I think they're planning to introduce it into schools."

"They're mad. What you've got to teach people is to read slowly. And not to fidget about so much. And do you know why they invent all these things? Because they're scared. People are scared to pause on things, because that compromises them. That's why they flee the country and move to the cities. They're scared of being by themselves."

"Yes, the world's full of fear."

"And those with power exploit that fear. Individual life has never been so despised or authority so revered."

"Sure, it's easier to live as one, to decide as one. Even dying's easier, if you die at someone else's expense. We're invaded by fear. There's the common man's fear, and he hands himself over to the strong man. But there's also the fear the powerful feel; they don't dare to stay alone. Because they're scared, they cling onto power."

"Here people abandon the country to go work in factories. And when they come back they don't like the country anymore. The country's hard. You've always got to be alert, and you're responsible for everything and not just for a part, like in a factory."

"What's more, the country's the experience of solitude. You can't go to the films, or take refuge in a bar."

"Exactly. It's the experience of being free. It's like poetry. Life's like poetry, when the poet writes a poem. It begins as an invitation to the unknown: the first line gets written and what's to follow is unknown. It's unsure whether in the next line poetry's waiting for us, or failure. And that sense of mortal danger accompanies the poet in all his adventures."

"In each verse a decision awaits us, and we can't choose to close our eyes and let instinct work on its own. Poetic instinct consists of an alert tension."

"In each line, in each phrase the possibility of failure is concealed. The possibility that the whole poem, not just that isolated verse, will fail. That's how life is: at every moment we can lose it. Every moment there's mortal risk. Each instant is a choice."

"You're right. Poetry is the experience of liberty. The poet risks himself, chances all on the poem's all with each verse he writes."

"And you can't change your mind. Each act, each verse is

irrevocable, forever. In each verse one is committed forever. But now folks have become irresponsible. No one wants to decide for himself. Like those poets who copy their ancestors."

"Don't you believe in the tradition?"

"Yes, but each poet's born to express something that's his own. And his first duty is to deny his ancestors, the rhetoric of those who've come before. When I started writing I found that the words of the old writers were no use to me; it was necessary for me to create my own language. And that language—which surprised and troubled some people—was the language of my community, the language that surrounded my childhood and adolescence. I had to wait a long time before I found my words. You've got to use everyday language. . . ."

"But subjected to a different pressure. As if each word had been created only to express that particular moment. Because there's a certain fatality in words; a French writer says that 'images can't be looked for, they're found.' I don't think he means that chance presides over creation but that a *fated choice* leads us to certain words."

"The poet creates his own language. Then he ought to fight against *that* rhetoric. He should never abandon himself to his style."

"There are no poetic styles. When you get to style, literature displaces poetry."

"That was the case with American poetry when I started writing. That's where all my difficulties and my successes began. And now maybe it's necessary to fight against the rhetoric we've made. The world goes round and what was in yesterday is out today. You've got to make a little fun of all this. No need to take anything too seriously, not even ideas. Or rather, precisely because we're so serious and passionate, we ought to laugh at ourselves a little. Don't trust those who don't know how to laugh."

And he laughed with the laughter of a man who has seen rain, and also of a man who has got wet. We got up and went out for a little walk. We went down the hill. The dog leapt ahead of us. As we came out, he said to me:

"Most of all, don't trust those who don't know how to laugh at themselves. Solemn poets, humorless professors, prophets who only know how to howl and harangue. All those dangerous men."

"Do you read the contemporaries?"

"I always read poetry. I like reading the poems of young writers. And some philosophers. But I can't stand novels. I don't think I've ever read one through."

We walked on. When we got to the farmhouse, the children gathered round us. The poet was now telling me about his childhood, the years in San Francisco, and his return to New England.

"This is my country and I believe this is where the nation has its roots. Everything grew from here. Do you know that the state of Vermont refused to participate in the war against Mexico? Yes, everything grew from here. This is where the desire to immerse oneself in the unknown began, and the desire to stay alone with yourself. We ought to go back to that if we want to preserve what we are."

"It seems pretty hard to me. You're now a rich people."

"Years ago I thought of going to a little country, where the noise that everyone makes just isn't heard. I chose Costa Rica; when I was getting ready to go I learned that there too an American company called the tune. I didn't go. That's why I'm here, in New England."

We came to the turning. I looked at my watch: more than two hours had passed.

"I'd better be going. They're waiting for me down below, in Bread Loaf."

He stretched out his hand.

"You know the way?"

"Yes," I said, and we shook hands. When I'd gone a few steps I heard his voice:

"Come back soon! And when you get to New York, write to me. Don't forget."

I answered with a nod. I saw him climbing the path playing with his dog. "And he's seventy years old," I thought. As I walked back, I remembered another loner, another visit. "I think Robert Frost would like to have known Antonio Machado. But how would they have understood each other? The Spaniard didn't speak English, and the American doesn't know Spanish. No matter, they would have smiled. I'm sure they would have made friends straightaway." I remembered the house at Rocafort, in Valencia, the wild, neglected garden, the living room and the dust-covered furniture. And Machado, the cigarette in his mouth gone out. The Spaniard was also an old man retired from the world, and he too knew how to laugh and he too was absentminded. Like the American, he liked to philosophize, not in the schools but at the periphery. Sages for the people; the American in his cabin, the Spaniard in his provincial café. Machado too expressed a horror of the solemn and had the same smiling gravity. "Yes, the Anglo-Saxon has the cleaner shirt and there are more trees in his view. But the other's smile was sadder and finer. There's a great deal of snow in this fellow's poems, but there's dust, antiquity, history in the other's. That dust of Castile, that dust of Mexico, which as soon as you touch it dissolves between your hands. . . ."

Vermont, June 1945

WALT WHITMAN

Walt Whitman is the only great modern poet who does not seem to experience discord when he faces his world. Not even solitude; his monologue is a universal chorus. No doubt there are at least two people in him: the public poet and the private person who conceals his true erotic inclinations. But the mask—that of the poet of democracy—is rather more than a mask; it is his true face. Despite certain recent interpretations, in Whitman the poetic and the historical dream come together. There is no gap between his beliefs and social reality. And this fact is more important—I mean, more widely pertinent and significant—than any psychological consideration. The uniqueness of Whitman's poetry in the modern world cannot be explained except as a function of another, even greater, uniqueness which includes it: that of America.

In a book* which is a model of its genre, Edmundo O'Gorman has shown that our continent was never discovered. In effect, it is impossible to discover something which does not exist, and America, before its so-called discovery, did not exist. One ought rather to speak of the *invention* of America than of its discovery. If America is a creation of the European spirit, it begins to emerge from the sea-mists centuries before the expeditions of Columbus. And what the Europeans discover when they reach these lands is their own historic dream. Reyes has devoted some lucid pages to this subject: America is a sudden embodiment of a European utopia. The dream becomes a reality, a present; America is a present: a gift, a given of history. But it is an open present, a today that is tinged with tomorrow. The presence and the present of America are a future; our continent is, by its nature, the land which does not exist on its own, but as something which is created and invented. Its being, its reality or substance, consists of being always future, history which is justified not by the past but by what is to come. Our foundation is not what America was but what it will be. America never was; and *it is, only if it is utopia*, history on its way to a golden age.

This may not be entirely true if one considers the colonial period of Spanish and Portuguese America. But it is revealing how, just as soon as the Latin Americans acquire self-consciousness and oppose the Spaniards, they rediscover the utopian nature of America and make the French utopias their own. All of them see in wars of independence a return to first principles, a reversion to what America really is. The War of Independence is a correction of American history and, as such, a restoration of the original reality. The exceptional and genuinely paradoxical nature of this restoration becomes clear if one notes that it consists of a restoration of the future. Thanks to French revolutionary principles,

La idea del descubrimiento de America (1951)

9

Latin America becomes again what it was at its birth: not a past, but a future, a dream. The dream of Europe, the place of choice, spatial and temporal, of all that the European reality could not be except by denying itself and its past. America is the dream of Europe, now free of European history, free of the burden of tradition. Once the problem of independence is resolved, the abstract and utopian nature of liberal America begins to show again in episodes such as the French intervention in Mexico. Neither Juárez nor his soldiers ever believed—according to Cosío Villegas—that they fought against France, but against a French usurpation. The true France was ideal and universal and more than just a nation, it was an idea, a philosophy. Cuesta says, with some justice, that the war with the French should be seen as a "civil war." It needed the Mexican Revolution to wake the country from this philosophical dream—which, in another way, concealed an historical reality hardly touched upon by the Independence, the Reform, and the Dictatorship—and discover itself, no longer as an abstract future but as an origin in which the three times needed to be sought: our past, our present, our future. The historical emphasis changed tense, and in this consists the true spiritual significance of the Mexican Revolution.

The utopian character of America is even purer in the Saxon portion of the continent. There were no complex Indian cultures there, nor did Roman Catholicism erect its vast nontemporal structures: America was—if it was anything—geography, pure space, open to human action. Lacking historical substance—old class divisions, ancient institutions, inherited beliefs and laws—reality presented only natural obstacles. Men fought, not against history, but against nature. And where there was an historical obstacle—as in the Indian societies—it was erased from history and, reduced to a mere act of nature, action followed as if this were so. The North American attitude can be condemned in these terms: all that does not have a part in the utopian nature of America does not properly belong to history: it is a natural event and, thus, it doesn't exist; or it exists only as an inert obstacle, not as an alien conscience. Evil is outside, part of the natural world—like Indians, rivers, mountains, and other obstacles which must be domesticated or destroyed; or it is an intrusive reality (the English past, Spanish Catholicism, monarchy, etc.). The American War of Independence is the expulsion of the intrusive elements, alien to the American essence. If American reality is the reinvention of itself, whatever is found in any way irreducible or unassimilable is not American. In other places the future is a human attribute: because we are men, we have a future; in the Anglo-Saxon America of the last century, the process is inverted and the future determines man: we are men because we have a future. And whatever has no future is not man. Thus, reality leaves no gap at all for contradiction, ambiguity, or conflict to appear.

Whitman can sing confidently and in blithe innocence about democracy militant because the American utopia is confused with and indistinguishable from American reality. Whitman's poetry is a great prophetic dream, but it is a dream within another even greater one that feeds it. America is dreamed in Whitman's poetry because it is a dream itself. And it is dreamed as a concrete reality, almost a *physical* reality, with its men, its rivers, its cities and mountains. All that huge mass of reality moves lightly, as if it were weightless; and in fact, it is without historic weight: it is the future incarnate. The reality Whitman sings is utopian. By this I do not mean that it is unreal or exists only as idea, but that its essence, what enlivens it, justifies and makes sense of its progress and gives weight to its movements, is the future. Dream within a dream, Whitman's poetry is realistic only on this count: his dream is the dream of the reality itself, which has no other substance but to invent itself and dream itself. "When we dream that we dream," Novalis says, "waking is near at hand." Whitman was never aware that he dreamed and always thought himself a poetic realist. And he was, but only insofar as the reality

11

he celebrated was not something given, but a substance crossed and recrossed by the future.

America dreams itself in Whitman because it was itself a dream, pure creation. Before and since Whitman we have had other poetic dreams. All of them—whether the dreamer's name is Poe or Darío, Melville or Dickinson—are more like attempts to escape from the American nightmare.

Mexico, 1956

William Carlos Williams: The Saxifrage Flower

for James Laughlin

In the first third of our century, a change occurred in the literatures of the English language which affected verse and prose, syntax and sensibility, imagination and prosody alike. The change—similar to those which occurred about the same time in other parts of Europe and in Latin America—was originally the work of a handful of poets, almost all of them Americans. In that group of founders, William Carlos Williams occupies a place at once central and unique: unlike Pound and Eliot, he preferred to bury himself in a little city outside New York rather than uproot himself and go to London or Paris; unlike Wallace Stevens and e. e. cummings, who also decided to stay in the United States but who were cosmopolitan spirits, Williams from the outset sought a poetic Americanism. In effect, as he explains in the beautiful essays of *In the American Grain* (1925), America is not a given reality but something we all make together with our hands, our eyes, our brains, and our lips. The American reality is material, mental, visual, and above all, verbal: whether he speaks Spanish, English, Portuguese, or French, American man speaks a language different from the European original. More than just a reality we discover or make, America is a reality we speak.

William Carlos Williams was born in Rutherford, New Jersey, in 1883. His father was English, his mother Puerto Rican. He studied medicine at the University of Pennsylvania. There he met Pound—a friendship that was to last throughout his life—and the poet H. D. (Hilda Doolittle), who fascinated the two young poets. After taking his doctorate and a short period of pediatric study in Leipzig, in 1910 he settled definitively in Rutherford. Two years later he married Florence Herman: a marriage that lasted a lifetime. Also for a lifetime he practiced a double vocation: medicine and poetry. Though he lived in the provinces, he was not a provincial: he was immersed in the artistic and intellectual currents of our century, traveled on various occasions to Europe, and befriended English, French, and Latin American writers. His literary friendships and enmities were varied and intense: Pound, Marianne Moore, Wallace Stevens, Eliot (whom he admired and condemned), e. e. cummings, and others, younger, like James Laughlin and Louis Zukofsky. His influence and friendship were decisive on Allen Ginsberg and also on the poetry of Robert Creeley, Robert Duncan, and the English poet Charles Tomlinson. (Poetic justice: a young English poet—and very English—praised by one who practiced almost his whole life a kind of poetic anti-Anglicism and who never tired of saying that the American language wasn't really English.) In 1951 he suffered his first attack of paralysis but survived a dozen years, dedicated to a literary program of rare fecundity: books of poetry, a translation of Quevedo, memoirs, lectures, and readings of his poems across the whole country. He died on 4 March 1963, where he was born and spent his life: in Rutherford.

His work is vast and varied: poetry, fiction, essays, theater, autobiography. The poetry has been collected in four volumes: *Collected Earlier Poems* (1906–1939), *Collected Later Poems* (1940–1946), *Pictures from Breughel* (1950–1962), and *Paterson* (1946–1958), a long poem in five books. Also there is a slim book of prose-poems which sometimes make one think of the automatic writing Breton and Soupault were engaged in around this time: *Kora in Hell* (1920). But in taking over a poetic form invented by French poetry, Williams changes it and converts it into a method of exploring language and the varied strata of the collective unconscious. *Kora in Hell* is a book which could only have been written by an American poet and ought to be read from the perspective of a later book which is the axis of Williams's Americanism, his *ars poetica: In the American Grain.* I will not consider his novels, stories, or theater pieces. Suffice it to say that they are extensions and irradiations of his poetry. The boundary between prose and verse, always hard to draw, becomes very tenuous in this poet: his free verse is very close to prose, not as written but as spoken, the everyday language; and his prose is always rhythmic, like a coast bathed by poetic surf—not verse but the verbal flux and reflux that gives rise to verse.

From the time he started writing, Williams evinced a distrust of ideas. It was a reaction against the symbolist aesthetic shared by the majority of poets at that time (remember López Velarde) and in which, in his case, American pragmatism was combined with his medical profession. In a famous poem he defines his search: "To compose: not ideas but in things." But things are always beyond, on the other side: the "thing itself" is untouchable. Thus Williams's point of departure is not things but sensation. And yet sensation in turn is formless and instantaneous; one cannot build or do anything with pure sensations: that would result in chaos. Sensation is amphibious: at the same time it joins us to and divides us from things. It is the door through which we enter into things but also through which we come out of them and realize that we are not things. In order for sensation to accede to the objectivity of things it must itself be changed into a thing. The agent of change is language: the sensations are turned into verbal objects. A poem is a verbal object in which two contradictory properties are fused: the liveliness of the sensation and the objectivity of things.

Sensations are turned into verbal objects by the operation of a force which for Williams is not essentially distinct from electricity, steam, or gas: imagination. In some reflections written down in 1923 (included among the poems in the late edition of *Spring and All* as "dislocated prose"), Williams says that the imagination is "a creative force which makes objects." The poem is not a double of the sensation or of the thing. Imagination does not represent: it produces. Its products are poems, objects which were not real before. The poetic imagination produces poems, pictures, and cathedrals as nature produces pines, clouds, and crocodiles. Williams wrings the neck of traditional aesthetics: art does not imitate nature: it imitates its creative processes. It does not copy its products but its modes of production. "Art is not a mirror to reflect nature but imagination competes with the compositions of nature. The poet becomes a nature and works like her." It is incredible that Spanish-language critics have not paused over the extraordinary similarity between these ideas and those that Vicente Huidobro proclaimed in statements and manifestos. True, it's a matter of ideas that appear in the work of many poets and artists of that time (for example, in Reverdy, who initiated Huidobro into modern poetry), but the similarity between the North American and Latin American are impressive. Both *invert* in almost the same terms the Aristotelian aesthetic and *convert* it for the modern era: imagination is, like electricity, a form of energy, and the poet is the transmitter.

The poetic theories of Williams and the "Creationism" of Huidobro are twins, but hostile twins. Huidobro sees in poetry something homologous with magic and, like a primitive shaman who *makes* rain, wants to make poetry; Williams conceives of poetic imagination as an activity that completes and rivals science. Nothing is further from magic than Williams. In a moment of childish egotism, Huidobro said: "The poet is a little God," an expression that the American poet would have rejected. Another difference: Huidobro tried to produce verbal objects which were not imitations of real objects and which even negated them. Art as a means of escaping reality. The title of one of his books is also a definition of his purpose: *Horizonte cuadrado* (*Square Horizon*). Attempting the impossible: one need only compare the pictures of abstract painters with the images which microscopes and telescopes provide us to realize that we cannot get away from nature. For Williams the artist—it is significant that he was supported and inspired by the example of Juan Gris—*separates* the things of the imagination from the things of reality: cubist reality is not the table, the cup, the pipe, and the newspaper as they are but *another* reality, no less real. This *other* reality does not deny the reality of real things: it is *another* thing which is *the same thing* at the same time. "The mountain and the sea in a picture by Juan Gris," Williams says, "are not the mountain and the sea but a painting of the mountain and the sea." The poem-thing isn't the thing: it is something else which exchanges signs of intelligence with the thing.

The non-imitative realism of Williams brings him close to two other poets: Jorge Guillén and Francis Ponge. (Again, I am pointing out coincidences, not influences.) A line of Guillén's defines their common repugnance for symbols: "the little birds chirp without design of grace." Do design and grace disappear? No: they enter the poem surreptitiously, without the poet's noticing. The "design of grace" is no longer in the real birds but in the text. The poem-thing is as unattainable as the poem-idea of symbolist poetry. Words are things, but things which mean. We cannot do away with meaning without doing away with the signs, that is, with language itself. Moreover: we would have to do away with the universe. All the things man touches are impregnated with meaning. Perceived by man, things exchange being for meaning: they are not, they mean. Even "having no meaning" is a way of meaning. The absurd is one of the extremes that meaning reaches when it examines its conscience and asks itself, What is the meaning of meaning? Ambivalence of meaning: it is the fissure through which we enter things and the fissure through which being escapes from them.

Meaning ceaselessly undermines the poem; it seeks to reduce its reality as an object of the senses and as a unique thing to an idea, a definition, or a "message." To protect the poem from the ravages of meaning, poets stress the material aspect of language. In poetry, the physical properties of the sign, audible and visible, are not less but more important than the semantic properties. Or rather: meaning returns to sound and becomes its servant. The poet works on the nostalgia which the signified feels for the signifier. In Ponge this process is achieved by the constant play between prose and poetry, fantastic humor and common sense. The result is a new being: the *objeu*. All the same, we can make fun of meaning, disperse and pulverize it, but we cannot annihilate it: whole or in living fragments and wriggling, like the slices of a serpent, meaning reappears. The creative description of the world turns, on the one hand, into a criticism of the world (Ponge as moralist); on the other, into *proeme* (the *précieux* Ponge, a sort of Gracián of objects). In Guillén the celebration of the world and of things results in history, satire, elegy: again, meaning. Williams's solution to the amphibious nature of language—words are things and are meanings—is different. He is not a European with a history behind him ready made but one ahead and to be made. He does not correct poetry with the morality of prose or convert humor into a teacher of resignation in song. On the contrary: prose is a ground where poetry grows, and humor is the spur of the imagination. Williams is a sower of poetic seeds.

The American language is a buried seed which can only come to fruition if irrigated and shone upon by poetic imagination.

Partial reconciliation, always partial and provisional, between meaning and thing. Meaning—criticism of the world in Guillén, of language in Ponge—becomes in Williams an active power at the service of things. Meaning *makes*, is the midwife of objects. His art seeks "to reconcile people and stones through metaphor," American man and his landscape, speaking being with mute object. The poem is a metaphor in which objects speak and words cease to be ideas to become sensible objects. Eye and ear: the object heard and the word drawn. In connection with the first, Williams was the master and friend of the so-called Objectivists: Zukofsky, Oppen; in connection with the second, of the Black Mountain school: Olson, Duncan, Creeley. Imagination not only sees: it hears; not only hears: it says. In his search for the American language, Williams finds (hears) the basic measure, a meter of variable foot but with a triadic accentual base. "We know nothing," he says, "but the dance: the measure is all we know." The poem-thing is a verbal object, rhythmical. Its rhythm is a transmutation of the language of a people. By means of language Williams makes the leap from thing and sensation to the world of history.

Paterson is the result of these concerns. Williams goes from the poem-thing to the poem-as-system-of-things. Single and multiple system: single as a city were it one man only, multiple as a woman were she many flowers. *Paterson* is the biography of a city of the industrial East of the United States and the history of one man. City and man are fused in the image of a waterfall that cascades down, with a deafening roar, from the stone mouth of the mountain. Paterson has been founded at the foot of that mountain. The cataract is language itself, the people who never know what they say and who wander always in search of the meaning of what they say. Cataract and mountain, man and woman, poet and people, preindustrial and industrial age, the incoherent noise of the cascade and the search for a measure, a meaning. *Paterson* belongs to the poetic *genre* invented by modern American poetry which oscillates between the *Aeneid* and a treatise on political economy, the *Divine Comedy* and journalism: huge collections of fragments, the most imposing example of which is Pound's *Cantos*.

All these poems, obsessed as much by a desire to *speak* the American reality as to *make* it, are the contemporary descendants of Whitman, and all of them, one way or another, set out to fulfill the prophecy of *Leaves of Grass*. And in a sense they do fulfill it, but negatively. Whitman's theme is the embodiment of the future in America. Marriage of the concrete and the universal, present and future: American democracy is the universalizing of national-bound European man and his rerooting in a particular land and society. The particularity consists in the fact that that society and that place are not a tradition but a present fired toward the future. Pound, Williams, and even Hart Crane are the other side of this promise: their poems demonstrate to us the ruins of that project. Ruins no less grand and impressive than the others. Cathedrals are the ruins of Christian eternity, *stupas* are the ruins of Buddhist vacuity, the Greek temples of the *polis* and of geometry, but the big American cities and their suburbs are the living ruins of the future. In those huge industrial wastebins the philosophy and morality of progress have come to a standstill. With the modern world ends the titanism of the future, compared with which the titanisms of the past—Incas, Romans, Chinese, Egyptians—seem childish sand castles.

Williams's poem is complex and uneven. Beside magical or realistic fragments of great intensity, there are long disjointed chunks. Written in the face of and sometimes against *The Waste Land* and the *Cantos*, it gets out of hand in its polemic with these two works. This is its principal limitation: reading it depends on other readings, so that the reader's judgment turns fatally to comparison. The vision Pound and Eliot had of the modern world was somber. Their pessimism was instinct with feudal nostalgias and precapitalist concepts; thus their just condemnation of money and modernity turned immediately into conservative and, in Pound's case, Fascist attitudes. Though Williams's vision is not optimistic either—how could it be?—there are in it no reminiscences of other ages. This could be an advantage, but it is not: Williams has no philosophic or religious system, no coherent collection of ideas and beliefs. What his immediate tradition (Whitman) offered him was unusable. There is a kind of void at the center of Williams's conception (though not in his short poems) which is the very void of contemporary American culture. The Christianity of *The Waste Land* is a truth that has been burned, calcined, and which, in my view, will not put out leaves again, but it was a central truth which, like light from a dead star, still *touches* us. I find nothing like that in *Paterson.* Comparison with the *Cantos* is not to Williams's advantage either. The United States is an imperial power, and if Pound could not be its Virgil he was at least its Milton: his theme is the fall of a great power. The United States gained a world but lost its soul, its future—that universal future in which Whitman believed. Perhaps on account of his very integrity and morality, Williams did not see the imperial aspect of his country, its demonic dimension.

Paterson has neither the unity nor the religious authenticity of *The Waste Land*—even if Eliot's religious feeling is negative. The *Cantos,* for their part, are an incomparably vaster and richer poem than Williams's, one of the few contemporary texts that stand up to our terrible age. So what? The greatness of a poet is not measured by the extent but by the intensity and perfection of his works. Also by their liveliness. Williams is the author of the *liveliest* modern American poems. Yvor Winters rightly says, "Herrick is less great than Shakespeare but probably he is no less fine and will last as long as he. . . . Williams will be almost as indestructible as Herrick; at the end of this century we will see him recognized, along with Wallace Stevens, as one of the two best poets of his generation." The prophecy came true before Winters expected it to. As to his ideas about New World poetry— is he really the most American of the poets of his age? I neither know nor care. On the other hand, I know he is the freshest, the most limpid. Fresh like a flow of drinking water, limpid as that same water in a glass jug on an unpolished wooden table in a whitewashed room in Nantucket. Wallace Stevens once called him "a sort of Diogenes of contemporary poetry." His lantern, burning in full daylight, is a little sun of his own light. The sun's double and its refutation: that lantern illuminates areas forbidden to natural light.

In the summer of 1970, at Churchill College, Cambridge, I translated six Williams poems. Later, on two escapades, one to Veracruz and another to Zihuatanejo, I translated others. Mine are not literal translations: literalness is not only impossible but reprehensible. Nor are they (I wish they were!) re-creations: they are approximations and, at times, transpositions. What I most regret is that I was unable to find in Spanish a rhythm equivalent to Williams's. But rather than embroil myself in the endless subject of poetry translation, I prefer to tell how I met him. Donald Allen sent me an English version of a poem of mine ("Hymn Among Ruins"). The translation impressed me for two reasons: it was magnificent, and its author was William Carlos Williams. I vowed that I would meet him, and on one of my trips to New York I asked Donald Allen to take me with him, as he had taken me before to meet cummings. One afternoon we visited him at his house in Rutherford. He was already half-paralyzed. The house was built of wood, as is common in the United States, and it was more a doctor's than a writer's house. I have never met a less affected man—the opposite of an oracle. He was possessed by poetry, not by his role as a poet. Wit, calmness, that not taking yourself seriously which Latin American writers so lack. In each

French, Italian, Spanish, and Latin American writer—especially if he is an atheist and revolutionary—a clergyman is concealed; among the Americans plainness, sympathy, and *democratic* humanity—in the true sense of this word—break the professional shell. It has always surprised me that in a world of relations as hard as that of the United States, cordiality constantly springs out like water from an unstanchable fountain. Maybe this has something to do with the religious origins of American democracy, which was a transposition of the religious community to the political sphere and of the closed space of the Church to the open space of the public square. Protestant religious democracy preceded political democracy. Among us democracy was anti-religious in origin and from the outset tended not to strengthen society in the face of government, but government in the face of the Church.

Williams was less talkative than cummings, and his conversation induced you to love him rather than admire him. We talked of Mexico and of the United States. As is natural we fell into talking about roots. For us, I told him, the profusion of roots and pasts smothers us, but you are oppressed by the huge weight of the future which is crumbling away. He agreed and gave me a pamphlet which a young poet had just published with a preface written by him: it was *Howl* by Allen Ginsberg. I saw him again years later, shortly before his death. Though ill health had battered him hard, his temper and his brain were intact. We spoke again of the three or four or seven Americas: the red, the white, the black, the green, the purple. . . . Flossie, his wife, was with us. As we talked I thought of "Asphodel," his great love poem in age. Now, when I recall that conversation and write this, in my mind I pick the colorless flower and breathe its fragrance. "A strange scent," the poet says, "a *moral* scent." It is not really a scent at all, "except for the imagination." Isn't that the best definition of poetry: a language which does not say anything except to the imagination? In another poem too he says: "Saxifrage is my flower that splits open rocks." Imaginary flowers which work on reality, instant bridges between men and things. Thus the poet makes the world habitable.

Zihuatanejo, 20 January 1973

THE GRAPHICS OF CHARLES TOMLINSON: BLACK AND WHITE

When I first read one of Charles Tomlinson's poems, over ten years ago, I was struck by the powerful presence of an element which, later, I found in almost all his creative work, even in the most reflective and self-contemplating: the outer world, a presence at once constant and invisible. It is everywhere but we do not see it. If Tomlinson is a poet for whom "the outer world exists," it must be added that it does not exist for him as an independent reality, apart from us. In his poems the distinction between subject and object is attenuated until it becomes, rather than a frontier, a zone of interpenetration, giving precedence not to the subject but to the object: the world is not a representation of the subject—the subject is the projection of the world. In his poems, outer reality—more than merely the space in which our actions, thoughts, and emotions unfold—is a climate which involves us, an impalpable substance, at once physical and mental, which we penetrate and which penetrates us. The world turns to air, temperature, sensation, thought; and we become stone, window, orange peel, turf, oil stain, helix.

Against the idea of the world-as-spectacle, Tomlinson opposes the concept—a very English one—of the world as event. His poems are neither a painting nor a description of the object or its more or less constant properties; what interests him is the process which leads it to be the object that it is. He is fascinated—with his eyes open: a lucid fascination—at the universal busyness, the continuous generation and degeneration of things. His is a poetry of the minimal catastrophes and resurrections of which the great catastrophe and resurrection of the world is composed. Objects are unstable congregations ruled alternately by the forces of attraction and repulsion. Process and not transition: not the place of departure and the place of arrival but what we are when we depart and what we have become when we arrive. . . . The water-drops on a bench wet with rain, crowded on the edge of a slat, after an instant of ripening—analogous in the affairs of men to the moment of doubt which precedes major decisions—fall on to the concrete; "dropped seeds of now becoming then." A moral and physical evocation of the water-drops. . . .

Thanks to a double process, at once visual and intellectual, the product of many patient hours of concentrated passivity and of a moment of decision, Tomlinson can isolate the object, observe it, leap suddenly inside it, and, before it dissolves, take the snapshot. The poem is the perception of the change, a perception which includes the poet: he changes with the changes of the object and perceives himself in the perception of those changes. The leap into the object is a leap into himself. The mind is a photographic darkroom; there the images—"the gypsum's snow / the limestone stair / and boneyard landscape grow / into the identity of flesh" ("The Cavern"). It is not, of course, a pantheistic claim of being everywhere and being everything. Tomlinson does not wish to be the heart and soul of the universe. He does not seek the "thing in itself" or the "thing in myself" but rather things in that moment of indecision when they are on the point of generation or degeneration. The moment they appear or disappear before us, before they form as objects in our minds or resolve in our forgetfulness. . . . Tomlinson quotes a passage from Kafka which defines his purpose admirably: "to catch a glimpse of things as they may have been before they show themselves to me."

His procedure approaches, at one extreme, science: maximum objectivity and purification, though not suppression, of the subject. On the other hand, nothing is further from modern scientism. This is not because of the aestheticism for which he is at times reproached, but because his poems are experiences and not experiments. Aestheticism is an affectation, contortion, preciosity, and in Tomlinson we find rigor, precision, economy, subtlety. The experiments of modern science are carried out on segments of reality, while experiences implicitly postulate that the grain of sand is a world and each fragment figures the whole; the archetype of experiments is the quantitative model of mathematics, while in experience a qualitative element appears which up to now has been rebel to measurement. A contemporary mathematician, René Thom, describes the situation precisely and gracefully: "A la fin du XVIIième siècle, la controverse faisait rage entre tenants de physique de Descartes et de Newton. Descartes, avec ses tourbillons, ses atomes crochus, etc., expliquait tout et ne calculait rien; Newton, avec la loi de gravitation en l/r^2, calculait tout et n'expliquait rien." And he adds, "Le point de vue newtonien se justifie pleinement par son efficacité . . . mais les esprits soucieux de compréhension n'auront jamais, au regard des théories qualitatives et descriptives, l'attitude méprisant du scientisme quantitatif." It is even less justifiable to undervalue the poets, who offer us not theories but experiences.

In many of his poems, Tomlinson presents us with the changes in the particle of dust, the outlines of the stain spreading on the

27

rag, the way the pollen's flying mechanism works, the structure of the whirlwind. The experience fulfills a need of the human spirit: to imagine what we cannot see, give ideas a form the senses can respond to, *see* ideas. In this sense the poet's experiences are not less truthful than the experiments carried out in our laboratories, though their truth is on another level from scientific truth. Geometry translates the abstract relationships between bodies into forms which are visible archetypes: thus it is the frontier between the qualitative and the quantitative. But there is another frontier: that of art and poetry, which translates into sensible forms, that are at the same time archetypes, the qualitative relationships between things and men. Poetry—imagination and sensibility made language—is a crystallizing agent of phenomena. Tomlinson's poems are crystals, produced by the combined action of his sensibility and his imaginative and verbal powers—crystals sometimes transparent, sometimes rainbow-colored, not all perfect, but all poems that we can look through. The act of looking becomes a destiny and a profession of faith: seeing is believing.

It is hardly surprising that a poet with these concerns should be attracted to painting. In general, the poet who turns to plastic work tries to express with shapes and colors those things he cannot say with words. The same is true of the painter who writes. Arp's poetry is a counterpointing of wit and fantasy set against the abstract elegance of his painting. In the case of Michaux, painting and drawing are essentially rhythmic incantations, signs beyond articulate language, visual magic. The expressionism of some of Tagore's ink drawings, with their violence, compensates us for the sticky sweetness of many of his melodies. To find one of Valéry's watercolors among the arguments and paradoxes of the *Cahiers* is like opening the window and finding that, outside, the sea, the sun, and the trees still exist. When I was considering Tomlinson, I called to mind these other artists, and I asked myself how this desire to paint came to manifest itself in a meditative temperament such as his—a poet whose main faculty of sense is his eyes, but eyes which think. Before I had a chance to ask him about this, I received, around 1970, a letter from him in which he told me he had sent me one of the *New Directions Anthologies*, which included reproductions of some of his drawings done in 1968. Later in 1970, during my stay in England, I was able to see other drawings from that same period—all of them in black and white, except for a few in sepia; studies of cow skulls, skeletons of birds, rats, and other creatures which he and his daughters had found in the countryside and on the Cornish beaches.

In Tomlinson's poetry, the perception of movement is exquisite and precise. Whether the poem is about rocks, plants, sand, insects, leaves, birds, or human beings, the true protagonist, the hero of each poem, is change. Tomlinson hears foliage grow. Such an acute perception of variations, at times almost imperceptible, in beings and things necessarily implies a vision of reality as a system of calls and replies. Beings and things, in changing, come in contact: change means relationship. In those Tomlinson drawings, the skulls of the birds, rats, and cows were isolated structures, placed in an abstract space, far from other objects, and even at a remove from themselves, fixed and immovable. Rather than a counterpointing of his poetic work, they seemed to me a contradiction. He missed out some of the features which attract me to his poetry: delicacy, wit, refinement of tones, energy, depth. How could he recover all these qualities without turning Tomlinson the painter into a servile disciple of Tomlinson the poet? The answer to this question is found in the work—drawings, collages, and *decalcomanía**—of recent years.

Tomlinson's painting vocation began, significantly, in a fas-

---

*"*Decalcomanía* without preconceived object or *decalcomanía* of desire: by means of a thick brush, spread out black gouache, more or less diluted in places, upon a sheet of glossy white paper, and cover at once with a second sheet, upon which exert an even pressure. Lift off the second sheet without haste"—Oscar Domínguez, quoted in *Surrealism* by Roger Cardinal and Robert Stuart Short.

cination with films. When he came down from Cambridge in 1948, he had not only seen "all the films"; he was also writing scripts which he sent to producers and which they, invariably, returned to him. This passion died out in time but left two enduring interests: the image in motion, and the idea of a literary text as support for the image. Both elements reappear in the poems and the collages. When the unions closed the doors of the film industry against him, Tomlinson dedicated himself energetically to painting. His first experiments, combining *frottage*, oil, and ink, date from that period. Between 1948 and 1950 he exhibited his work in London and Manchester. In 1951 he had the opportunity to live for a time in Italy. During that trip the urge to paint began to recede before the urge to write poetry. When he returned to England, he devoted himself more and more to writing, less and less to painting. In this first phase of his painting, the results were indecisive: *frottages* in the shadow of Max Ernst, studies of water and rocks more or less inspired by Cézanne, trees and foliage seen in Samuel Palmer rather than in the real world. Like other artists of his generation, he made the circuit round the various stations of modern art and paused, long enough to genuflect, before the geometric chapel of the Braques, the Légers, and the Grises. During those same years—getting on toward 1954—Tomlinson was writing the splendid *Seeing Is Believing* poems. He ceased painting.

The interruption was not long. Settled near Bristol, he returned to his brushes and crayons. The temptation to use black (why? he still asks himself) had an unfortunate effect: by exaggerating the contours, it made his compositions stiff. "I wanted to reveal the pressure of objects," he wrote to me, "but all I managed to do was thicken the outlines." In 1968 Tomlinson seriously confronted his vocation and the obstacles to it. I refer to his inner inhibitions and, most of all, to that mysterious predilection for black. As always happens, an intercessor appeared: Seghers. Tomlinson was wise to have chosen Hercules Seghers—each of us has the intercessors he deserves. It is worth noting that the work of this great artist—I am thinking of his impressive stony landscapes done in white, black, and sepia—also inspired Nicolas de Staël. Seghers's lesson is: Do not abandon black, do not resist it, but embrace it, walk around it as you walk around a mountain. Black was not an enemy but an accomplice. If it was not a bridge, then it was a tunnel: if he followed it to the end it would bring him through to the other side, to the light. Tomlinson had found the key which had seemed lost. With that key he unlocked the door so long bolted against him and entered a world which, despite its initial strangeness, he soon recognized as his own. In that world black ruled. It was not an obstacle but an ally. The ascetic black and white proved to be rich, and the limitation on the use of materials provoked the explosion of forms and fantasy.

In the earliest drawings of this period, Tomlinson began with the method which shortly afterward he was to use in his collages: he set the image in a literary context and thus built up a system of visual echoes and verbal correspondences. It was only natural that he should have selected one of Mallarmé's sonnets in which the sea snail is a spiral of resonances and reflections. The encounter with surrealism was inevitable—not to repeat the experiences of Ernst or Tanguy but to find the route back to himself. Perhaps it would be best to quote a paragraph of the letter I mentioned before: "Why couldn't I make their world my world? But in my own terms. In poetry I had always been drawn to impersonality—how could I go beyond the self in painting?" Or put another way: how to use the surrrealists' psychic automatism without lapsing into subjectivism? In poetry we accept the accident and use it even in the most conscious and premeditated works. Rhyme, for example, is an accident; it appears unsummoned, but, as soon as we accept it, it turns into a choice and a rule. Tomlinson asked himself: what in painting is the equivalent of rhyme in poetry? What is *given* in the visual arts? Oscar Domínguez answered that question with his *decalcomanía*. In fact, Domínguez was a bridge to an artist closer to Tomlinson's own sensibility. In those days he was obsessed by Gaudí, and by the memory of the dining-room windows in Casa Batlló. He drew them many times: what would happen if we could look out from these windows on the lunar landscape?

Those two impulses, Domínguez's *decalcomanía* and Gaudí's architectural arabesques, fused: "Then, I conceived of the idea of cutting and contrasting sections of a sheet of *decalcomanía* and fitting them into the irregular windowpanes. . . . Scissors! Here was the instrument of choice. I found I could *draw* with scissors, reacting *with* and *against* the *decalcomanía*. . . . Finally I took a piece of paper, cut out the shape of Gaudí's window and moved this mask across my *decalcomanía* until I found my moonscape. . . . The 18th of June 1970 was a day of discovery for me: I made my best arabesque of a mask, fitted it round a paint blot and then extended the idea of reflection implicit in the blot with geometric lines. . . ." Tomlinson had found, with different means from those he used in his poetry but with analogous results, a visual counterpoint for his verbal world: a counterpointing and a complement.

The quotes from Tomlinson's letter reveal with involuntary but overwhelming clarity the double function of the images, be they verbal or visual. Gaudí's windows, converted by Tomlinson into masks, that is, into objects which *conceal*, serve him to *reveal*. And what does he discover through those window-masks? Not the real world: an imaginary landscape. What began on the 18th of June 1970 was a fantastic morphology. A morphology and not a mythology: the places and beings which Tomlinson's collages evoke for us reveal no paradise or hell. Those skies and those caverns are not inhabited by gods or devils; they are places of the mind. To be more exact, they are places, beings, and things revealed in the darkroom of the mind. They are the product of the confabulation—in the etymological sense of that word—of accident and imagination.

Has it all been the product of chance? But what is meant by that word? Chance is never produced by chance. Chance possesses a logic—is a logic. Because we have yet to discover the rules of something, we have no reason to doubt that there are rules. If we could outline a plan, however roughly, of its involved corridors of mirrors which ceaselessly knot and unknot themselves, we would know a little more of what really matters. We would know something, for instance, about the intervention of "chance" both in scientific discoveries and artistic creation and in history and our daily life. Of course, like all artists, Tomlinson knows something: we ought to accept chance as we accept the appearance of an unsummoned rhyme.

In general, we should stress the moral and philosophical aspect of the operation: in accepting chance, the artist transforms a thing of fate into free choice. Or it can be seen from another angle: rhyme guides the text but the text produces the rhyme. A modern superstition is that of art as transgression. The opposite seems to me more exact: art transforms disturbance into a new regularity. Topology can show us something: the appearance of the accident provokes, rather than the destruction of the system, a recombination of the structure which was destined to absorb it. The structure validates the disturbance, art canonizes the exception. Rhyme is not a rupture but a binding agent, a link in the chain, without which the continuity of the text would be broken. Rhymes convert the text into a succession of auditory equivalences, just as metaphors make the poem into a texture of semantic equivalences. Tomlinson's fantastic morphology is a world ruled by verbal and visual analogies.

What we call chance is nothing but the sudden revelation of relationships between things. Chance is an aspect of analogy. Its unexpected advent provokes the immediate response of analogy, which tends to integrate the exception in a system of correspondences. Thanks to chance we discover that silence is milk, that the stone is composed of water and wind, that ink has wings and a beak. Between the grain of corn and the lion we sense no relationship at all, until we reflect that both serve the same lord: the sun. The spectrum of relationships and affinities between things is extensive, from the interpenetration of one object with another—"the sea's edge is neither sand nor water," the poem says—to the literary comparisons linked by the word *like*. Contrary to surrealist practice, Tomlinson does not juxtapose contradictory realities in order to produce a mental explosion. His method is more subtle. And his intention is distinct from theirs: he does not wish to alter reality but to achieve a modus vivendi with it. He is not certain that the function of imagination is to transform reality; he is certain, on the other hand, that it can make it more real. Imagination imparts a little more reality to our lives.

Spurred on by fantasy and reined in by reflection, Tomlinson's work submits to the double requirements of imagination and perception: one demands freedom and the other precision. His attempt seems to propose for itself two contradictory objectives: the saving of appearances, and their destruction. The purpose is not contradictory because what it is really about is the rediscovery—more precisely, the re-living—of the original act of making. The experience of art is one of the experiences of Beginning: that archetypal moment in which, combining one set of things with another to produce a new, we reproduce the very moment of the making of the worlds. Intercommunication between the letter and the image, the *decalcomanía* and the scissors, the window and the mask, those things which are hard-looking and those which are soft-looking, the photograph and the drawing, the hand and the compass, the reality which we see with our eyes and the reality which closes our eyes so that we see it: the search for a lost identity. Or as Tomlinson puts it best: "to reconcile the I that is with the I that I am." In the nameless, impersonal I that is are fused the I that measures and the I that dreams, the I that thinks and the I that breathes, the I which creates and the I which destroys.

Cambridge, Massachusetts, 1975

Jean-Paul Sartre:
A Memento

The death of Jean-Paul Sartre, after the initial shock this kind of news produces, aroused in me a feeling of resigned melancholy. I lived in Paris in the postwar years, which were the high noon of his glory and influence. Sartre bore that celebrity with humor and simplicity; despite the bigotry of many of his admirers which was irritating and funny at the same time, his simplicity, which was genuinely philosophical, disarmed more reticent spirits. During those years I read him with furious passion: one of his qualities was the way he could elicit from his readers, with the same violence, rejection and assent. Often, as I read, I lamented that I did not know him personally, so I might tell him face to face my doubts and disagreements. A chance incident gave me that opportunity.

A friend, sent to Paris by the University of Mexico to finish his philosophical studies, confided to me that he was in danger of losing his academic grant if he did not publish soon an article on some philosophical theme. It occurred to me that a conversation with Sartre might be the matter for that article. Through some common friends we got near to him and proposed our idea. He accepted it and a few days later the three of us dined in the bar of the Pont-Royal. The dinner interview lasted more than three hours, and during it Sartre was extremely lively, speaking with intelligence, passion, and energy. He also listened, and took the trouble to answer my questions and timid objections. My friend never wrote his article, but that first meeting gave me the opportunity to meet Sartre again at the same bar of the Pont-Royal. Our relationship ended after the third or fourth encounter: too many things divided us and I did not look him up again. I have defined these differences in some passages in my *Alternating Current* and *The Philanthropic Ogre*.

The subjects of those conversations were the topical ones of the time: existentialism and its relations with literature and politics. The publication in *Les temps modernes* of a fragment of the book on Genet which he was writing at the time led us to talk about that writer and about Saint Teresa. A parallel much to his liking since both, he said, in choosing Supreme Evil and Supreme Good ("le Non-Etre de l'Etre et l'Etre du non-Etre"), in fact had chosen the same thing. I was surprised that, guided only by a verbalist logic, he ignored precisely what was at the heart of his concerns and the foundation of his philosophical criticism: the subjectivity of Saint Teresa and her historical situation. In other words: the physical person that the Spanish nun had been, and the intellectual and affective horizon of her life, the religiosity of the Spanish sixteenth century. For Genet, Satan and God are words which signify cloudy realities, suprasensible entities: myths or ideas; for Saint Teresa, those same words were spiritual and sensible realities, incarnate ideas. And this is what distinguishes mystical from other expression: though the Devil is the Non-Person by substitution and though strictly, except in the mystery of the Incarnation, God is not a person either, for the believer both are tangible presences, humanized spirits. During that conversation I made an uncomfortable discovery: Sartre had not read Saint Teresa. He spoke on hearsay. Later, in newspaper statements, he said he had been inspired by a comedy of Cervantes, *El rufián dieboso*, in the writing of *Le Diable et le Bon Dieu*, though he made it clear he had not read the piece, only a summary. This ignorance of Spanish literature is not unusual but widespread among Europeans and Americans: Edmund Wilson vaingloriously proclaimed that he had read neither Cervantes nor Calderón nor Lope de Vega. Nevertheless, Sartre's confession reveals that he did not know one of the highest moments in European culture: the Spanish drama of the sixteenth and seventeenth centuries. His lack of curiosity still astonishes me, since one of the great themes of the Spanish theater, the source of some of the best works of Tirso de Molina, Mira de Amescua, and Calderón, is precisely the one which troubled him all his life: the conflict between grace and liberty. In another conversation he confided to me his admiration for Mallarmé. Years later, reading what he had written on this poet, I realized that once again the object of his admiration was not the poems which Mallarmé actually wrote but his project of absolute poetry, that Book he never made. Despite what his philosophy declares, Sartre always preferred shadows to realities.

Our last conversation was almost entirely about politics. Commenting on the discussions at the United Nations about the Russian concentration camps, he told me: "The British and the French have no right to criticize the Russians on account of their camps, since they've got their colonies. In fact, colonies are the concentration camps of the bourgeoisie." His sweeping moral judgment overlooked the specific differences—historic, social, political— between the two systems. In equating Western colonialism with the repressive Soviet system, Sartre fudged the issue, the only one that could and should interest an intellectual of the left such as he was: what was the true social and historic nature of the Soviet regime? By evading the basic theme, he helped indirectly those who wanted to perpetuate the lies with which, up to that time, Soviet reality had been masked. This was a serious equivocation, if one can so describe an intellectual and moral fault.

True, in those days imperialism exploited the colonial population as the Soviet system exploited the prisoners in the camps. The difference was that the colonies were not a part of the repressive system of bourgeois states (there were no French workers condemned to forced labor in Algeria, nor were there British dissidents deported to India), while the population of the camps consisted of the Soviet people themselves: farmers, workers, intellectuals, and whole social categories (ethnic, religious, and professional). The camps, that is to say, repression, were (are) an integral part of the Soviet system. In those years, moreover, the colonies achieved independence, while the system of concentration camps has spread, like an infection, into all the countries in which Communist regimes rule. And there is something more: is it even thinkable that in the Russian, Cuban, and Vietnamese camps movements of emancipation should arise and develop, movements like those that have liberated the old European colonies in Asia and Africa? Sartre was not insensible to these arguments, but it was hard to convince him: he thought that we bourgeois intellectuals had no right to criticize the vices of the Soviet system while in our own countries oppression and exploitation survived. When the Hungarian Revolution broke out, he attributed the uprising in part to Khrushchev's imprudent declarations revealing the crimes of Stalin: one ought not to upset the workers.

Sartre's case is exemplary but not unique. A sort of moralizing masochism, inspired by the best principles, has paralyzed a large number of European and Latin American intellectuals for more than thirty years. We have been educated in the double heritage of Christianity and the Enlightenment; both currents, religious and secular, in their highest development were critical. Our models have been those men who, like a Las Casas or a Rousseau, had the courage to tell and condemn the horrors and injustices of their own societies. I would not wish to betray that tradition; without it, our societies would cease to be that dialogue with themselves without which there is no real civilization and they would become a monologue of power, at once barbarous and monotonous. Criticism served Kant and Hume, Voltaire and Diderot, to establish the modern world. Their criticism and that of their heirs in the nineteenth century and the first half of the twentieth was creative. We have perverted criticism: we have put it at the service of our hatred of ourselves and of the world. We have not built anything with it, except prisons of concepts. Worst of all: with criticism we have justified tyrannies. In Sartre this intellectual sickness turned into an historical myopia: for him the sun of reality never shone. That sun is cruel but also, in some moments, it is a sun of plenitude and fortune. Plenitude, fortune: two words that do not appear in his vocabulary. . . . Our conversation ended abruptly: Simone de Beauvoir arrived and, rather impatiently, made him swallow down his coffee and depart.

Even though Sartre had made a brief trip to Mexico, he hardly spoke at all of his Mexican experience. I believe he was not a good traveler: he had too many opinions. His real journeys he took around himself, shut up in his room. Sartre's candor, his frankness and rectitude, impressed me as much as the solidity of his convictions. These two qualities were not at odds: his agility was that of a heavyweight boxer. He lacked grace but made up for it with a hearty, direct style. This lack of affectation was itself an affectation and could go beyond frankness to bluntness. Nonetheless, he welcomed the stranger cordially, and one guessed he was harsher with himself than with others. He was chubby and a little slow in movement; a round, unfinished face: more than a face, a ground plan of a face. The thick lenses of his spectacles made his person seem more remote. But one only had to hear him to forget his face. It's odd: though Sartre has written subtle pages on the meaning of the look and the act of looking, the effect of his conversation was quite the opposite; he annulled the power of sight.

When I recall those conversations I am surprised by the moral continuity, the constancy of Sartre: the themes and problems that impassioned him in his youth were those of his maturity and old age. He changed opinions often, yet, nevertheless, in all of his changes he remained true to himself. I remember I asked him if I was right to assume that the book on morality which he promised to write—a project he conceived as his great intellectual undertaking and which he never completed—would have to open out into a philosophy of history. He shook his head, doubtfully: the phrase "philosophy of history" seemed suspicious to him, spurious, as if philosophy was one thing and history another. Moreover, Marxism was already that philosophy, since it had penetrated to the core the sense of the historical movement of our time. He proposed within Marxism to insert the solid, real individual. We are our situation: our past, our moment; at the same time, we are something which cannot be reduced to those conditions, however much they determine us. In the introduction to *Les temps modernes* he speaks of a *total* liberation of man, but a few lines further on he says the danger consists in that "the man-totality" might disappear "swallowed up by class." Thus, he was opposed both to the ideology which reduces individuals to being nothing but functions of class, and to the one which conceived of classes as functions of the nation. He kept to this position throughout his life.

His philosophy of the "situation"—Ortega had said, more exactly, "circumstance"—did not seem to him a negation of the absolute but rather the only way to understand and realize it. In the same essay he said: "The absolute is Descartes, the man who eludes us because he has died, who lived in his epoch and pondered hour after hour with the means at hand, who loved in his

41

childhood a cross-eyed girl, etc.; what is relative is Cartesianism, that wandering philosophy which they trundle out century after century. . . ." I am not too sure that these peremptory statements would stand up to close scrutiny. Why must the "absolute" be a childhood passion for a cross-eyed girl (and why cross-eyed?) and why must the philosophy of Descartes (which is not exactly the Cartesianism Sartre depreciatingly alludes to) be relative beside that infantile passion? And why that word *absolute*, impregnated with theology? Neither passions nor philosophies are suited to that despotic adjective. There are passions for and toward the absolute and there are philosophies of the absolute but there are no passions or philosophies that are absolute. . . . I have digressed. What I wanted to stress is that in that essay Sartre introduces among the social and historical determinants an element of indeterminacy: the human person, people. Thus, back in 1947, he had begun his long and unhappy dialogue with Marxism and Marxists. What task did he really set himself? To reconcile communism and liberty. He failed, but his failure has been that of three generations of leftist intellectuals.

Sartre wrote philosophical treatises and philosophical essays, books of criticism and novels, stories and plays. Profusion is not excellence. His were not an artist's gifts: often he gets lost in useless digressions and amplifications. His language is insistent and repetitive: hammering as argument. The reader ends up exhausted, not convinced. If his prose is not memorable, what is to be said of his novels and stories? He wrote admirable narratives but he lacked a novelist's power: the ability to create worlds, atmospheres, and characters. The same criticism could be made of his plays: we remember the ideas of *Les mouches* and *Huis clos*, not the shadow-characters which express them. In his search for solid man Sartre time after time was left clutching a fistful of abstractions. And his philosophy? His contributions were valuable but partial. His work is not a beginning but a continuation and, at times, a commentary of others. What would be left of it without Heidegger?

In his essays lively, dense pages abound, always a little over-done, powerful verbal waves seething with ideas, sarcasm, things that just occurred to him. The best of his writing, to my taste, is the most personal, the least "committed," those texts which are closer to confession than to speculation, like so many pages of *Les mots*, perhaps his best book: the words embody, play, return to their childhood. Sartre excelled in two opposing modes: analysis and invective. He was an excellent critic and a fiery polemicist. The polemicist damaged the critic: his analyses often turned into accusations, as in his books on Baudelaire and Flaubert or in his wild critiques of surrealism. Worse than the polemicist's axe were the moralist's rod and the schoolmaster's ruler. Often Sartre exercised criticism like a tribunal that distributes punishments and admonishments exclusively. His *Baudelaire* is at the same time penetrating and partial; more than a study, it is a warning, a lecture. Though the book on Genet sins by the opposite excess— there are moments at which it is a very Christian apologia for abjection as a way to salvation—it has pages which are hard to forget. When Sartre allowed himself to be led by his verbal gift, the result was surprising. If in talking of men he reduced them to concepts, ideas, and theses, he still transformed words into animate beings. A cruel paradox: he despised literature and was above all else a literary man.

He thought and wrote much and on many things. In spite of this diversity, much that he said, even when he erred, seems to me essential. Let me state it differently: essential *for us*, his contemporaries. Sartre lived the ideas, the battles and tragedies of our age with the intensity with which others live out their private dramas. He was a conscience and a passion. The two words do not contradict each other because his was the conscience of a passion; I mean, conscience of the passing of time and of man.

More than a philosopher he was a moralist. Not in the sense of the traditions of the *Grand Siècle*, interested in the description and analysis of the soul and its passions. He was not a La Rochefoucauld. I call him moralist not on account of his psychological insight but because he had the courage to set himself throughout his life the only question which really matters: What reasons have we to live? Why and to what end do we live? Is it worthwhile living as we live?

We know the replies he gave to these questions: man, surrounded by nothing and non-sense, is little being. Man is not man: he is the project for man. That project is choice: we are condemned to choose, and our penalty is called history. We also know where that paradox of liberty as penalty led him. Time after time he supported the tyrannies of our century because he thought that the despotism of the revolutionary Caesars was nothing but the mask of liberty. Time after time he had to confess that he had erred: what seemed a mask was the concrete face of the Chiefs. In our century, revolution has been the mask of tyranny. Sartre saluted each triumphant revolution with joy (China, Cuba, Algeria, Vietnam) and afterward, always a little late, he had to declare that he had made a mistake: those regimes were abominable. If he was severe about the American intervention in Vietnam and the French policy in Algeria, he did not shut his eyes to the cases of Hungary, Czechoslovakia, and Cambodia. Nonetheless, for years he insisted on defending the Soviet Union and its satellites because he believed that, despite everything, those regimes embodied, even if in a deformed way, the socialist project. His criticism of the West was implacable and distills a hatred of his world and of himself; his preface to the book on Fanon is a fierce and impressive exercise in denigration which is, at the same time, a self-expiation. It is revealing that, in writing those pages, he did not perceive in the freedom movements of the so-called Third World the germs of political corruption which have transformed those revolutions into dictatorships.

Why did he strive so in order not to see and not to hear? I exclude of course the possibility of complicity or duplicity, as in the case of Aragon, Neruda, and so many others who, though they knew, kept silent. Obstinacy, pride? Penitential Christianity of a man who has ceased to believe in God but not in sin? Mad hope that one day things would change? But how *can* they change if no one dares denounce them, or if that denunciation, "so as not to play into the hands of imperialism," is conditioned and full of reservations and exonerating clauses? Sartre preached the responsibility of the writer, and, nonetheless, during the years when he exercised a kind of moral authority in the whole world (except the Communist countries), his successive and contradictory *engagements* were an example, if not of irresponsibility, then certainly of precipitateness and incoherence. The philosophy of "compromise" dissolved in contradictory public gestures. It is instructive to compare the changes in Sartre with the lucid and extremely coherent oeuvre of Cioran, a spirit apparently at the margins of our age but one who has lived and thought in depth and, for that reason, quietly. The ideas and attitudes of Sartre justified the opposite of what he set himself: the unembarrassed and generalized irresponsibility of the intellectuals on the left who during the last twenty years, in the name of revolutionary "compromise," tactics, dialectics, and other pretty terms, have eulogized and cloaked the tyrants and the executioners.

It would not be generous to continue with the catalogue of his obfuscations. How can we forget that they were the daughters of his love of liberty? Perhaps his love was not very clear-sighted on account of its very impetuous intensity. Moreover, many of those errors were ours: those of our age. At the end of his life he came around completely and joined up with his old adversary, Raymond Aron, in the campaign to charter a boat to transport the fugitives from the Communist tyranny of Vietnam. He also protested against the invasion of Afghanistan, and his name is one of those at the head of the manifesto of French intellectuals who petitioned their government to join the boycott of the Moscow Olympics. The shadows of Breton and Camus, whom he attacked with rage and little justice, should be satisfied. . . . The aberrations of Sartre are one more example of the perverse use of the Hegelian dialectic in the twentieth century. His influence has been lamentable on the European intellectual conscience: the dialectic makes us see evil as the necessary complement of the good. If all is in motion, evil is a moment of the good; but a *necessary* moment and, fundamentally, good: evil serves the good.

In a deeper layer of Sartre's personality there was an antique moral fund marked, more than by dialectics, by the familiar inheritance of Protestantism. Throughout his life he practiced with great severity the examination of conscience, axis of the spiritual life of his Huguenot ancestors. Nietzsche said that the great contribution of Christianity to the knowledge of the soul had been the invention of the examination of conscience and of its corollary, *remorse*, which is at the same time self-punishment and the exercise of introspection. The work of Sartre is a confirmation, yet another confirmation, of the precision of this idea. His criticism, whether of American politics or of the attitudes of Flaubert, follows the intellectual and moral scheme of the examination of conscience: it begins as a watchfulness, a tearing off of the veils and masks, not in search of nakedness but of the hidden ulcer, and it ends, inexorably, in a judgment. For the Protestant religious conscience, to know the world is to judge it and to judge it is to condemn it.

By a curious philosophical transposition, Sartre substituted for the predestination and liberty of Protestant theology psychoanalysis and Marxism. But all the great themes which fired the reformers appear in his work. The center of his thought was the complementary opposition between the situation (predestination) and liberty; this too was the theme of the Calvinists and the nub of their argument with the Jesuits. Not even God is absent: the Situation (History) assumes his functions, if not his features and his essence. But the Situation of Sartre is a deity which, since it has to have all the faces, has none: it is an abstract deity. Unlike the Christian God, it does not assume human form, nor is it an accomplice in our destiny: we are its accomplices and it is fulfilled in us. Sartre inherited from Christianity not transcendence, the affirmation of another reality and of another world, but the negation of this world and abhorrence of our earthly reality. Thus, in the depth of his analysis, protests, and insults against bourgeois society, the old vindictive voice of Christianity resounds. The true term for his criticism is *remorse*. In accusing his class and his world, Sartre accuses himself with the violence of a penitent.

It is remarkable that the two writers of greatest influence in France in this century—I am talking of moral, not literary, influence—have been André Gide and Jean-Paul Sartre. Two Protestants rebelling against Protestantism, their family, their class and its morality. Two moralist immoralists. Gide rebelled in the name of the senses and of the imagination; more than to liberate man, he wanted to free the shackled passions in each man. Communism disillusioned him because he perceived that it substituted for the Christian moral prison one more total and fierce. Gide was a moralist but also an aesthete, and in his work moral criticism is allied to the cultivation of the beautiful. The word *pleasure* has on his lips a savor at once subversive and voluptuous. More an evangelist than a radical, Sartre despised art and literature with the fury of a Church father. In a moment of desperation he said: "Hell is other people." A terrible expression, since the others are our horizon: the world of men. For this reason, no doubt, he later maintained that the liberation of the individual came by way of collective liberation. His work sets off from "I" to the conquest of "we." Perhaps he forgot that the "we" is a collective "thou": to love the others one must first love the other, the neighbor. We need, we moderns, to rediscover the "thou."

In one of his first works, *Les mouches*, there is a phrase which has been cited often but which is worth repeating: "Life begins the other side of despair." Only, what's on the other side of despair isn't life but the ancient Christian virtue we call hope. The first time the word *hope*, in an explicit way, appears on Sartre's lips is in the last interview which *Le nouvel observateur* published shortly before his death. It was his last statement. A disjointed and moving text. At one point, with an unbuttonedness which some have found disconcerting and others simply deplorable, he declares that his pessimism was a tribute to the fashion of the time. Strange affirmation: the whole interview is shot through with a vision of the world at times disillusioned and at others— most often—emphatically pessimistic. In the course of his conversation with his young disciple, Sartre reveals a stoical and admirable resignation in confronting his coming death. This attitude justly acquires all of its value because it stands out against a black backdrop: Sartre confesses that his work has remained incomplete, that his political action was frustrated, and that the world he leaves is more somber than the one he found at birth. For this reason I was genuinely impressed by his calm hope: despite the disasters of our age, one day men will reconquer (or will they conquer for the first time?) fraternity. I found it strange, on the other hand, that he should say that the origin and foundation of that hope is in Judaism. It is the least universal of the three monotheisms. Judaism is a closed fraternity. Why was he once again deaf to the voice of his tradition?

The dream of universal brotherhood—and more, the enlightened certainty that that is the state to which all men are naturally and supernaturally predestined, if we recover original innocence—appears in primitive Christianity. It reappears among the Gnostics of the third and fourth centuries and in the millennialist movements which, from time to time, have shaken the West, from the Middle Ages to the Reformation. But that little disagreement doesn't matter. It is uplifting that, at the end of his life, without rejecting his atheism, resigned to death, Sartre should have taken up the best and most pure element in our religious tradition: the vision of a world of men and women reconciled, transparent to each other because there is no longer anything to conceal or to fear, returned to an original nakedness. The loss and recovery of innocence were the theme of another great Protestant, involved as Sartre was in the battles of his century, and who, on account of the excess of his love for liberty, justified the tyrant Cromwell: John Milton. In the last book of *Paradise Lost* he describes the slow and distressing departure of Adam and Eve—and with them the departure of all of us, their children—toward the eventual innocent kingdom:

> The world was all before them, where to choose
> Their place of rest, and Providence their guide:
> They hand in hand, with wandering steps and slow,
> Through Eden took their solitary way.

When I wrote these pages and read through them, I thought once more of the man who inspired them. I was tempted to paraphrase him—homage and recognition—writing in his memory: *Liberty is other people.*

Mexico, April 1980

BAUDELAIRE AS ART CRITIC: PRESENCE AND PRESENT

In his first essay on the visual arts (the 1845 Salon), faced with a canvas that represents the emperor Marcus Aurelius at the moment when, about to die, he entrusts young Commodus to his Stoic friends, Baudelaire writes with characteristic impetuosity: "Here we see Delacroix in full, that is, we have before our eyes one of the most complete specimens of what genius can achieve in painting." A few lines further on, with one phrase, he gives the reason for his fascination with this historical-philosophical picture: "This heightening of the green and red pleases our soul." Not the theme nor the figures but the relation between two colors, one cool and the other warm. The presence which the painting summons up is not the historical or philosophical image but the accord between a blue and a flesh-hue, a yellow and a violet. The body and the soul—or the pagan and Christian traditions—reduced to a visual vibration: music for the eye. Ten years later, again considering the work of Delacroix, he is even more explicit and conclusive: "Above all one must emphasize, and this is very important, that seen from a great distance, a distance which makes it hard to analyze or even understand the subject, a Delacroix painting instantly produces on the soul a rich impression, happy or sad . . . it is as though this color—I beg pardon for these treacheries of language in expressing ideas of great delicacy—thinks for itself, independently of the objects it clothes." To see a picture is to hear it, to understand what it says. Painting, which is music, is also and above all else language.

The idea of language includes the idea of translation: the painter translates the word into visual images; the critic is a poet who translates lines and colors into words. The artist is the universal translator. True, that translation is a transmutation. This consists, as we know, of the interpretation of nonlinguistic signs by means of linguistic signs—or the reverse. Each of those "translations" is in fact another work, not so much a copy of as a metaphor for the original. Later I will touch on this theme; but here let me point out that Baudelaire, with the same vehemence with which he argues that analogy ("translation") is the only way of approaching the picture, insists that the color thinks, *independently* of the objects it clothes. My comments begin with an analysis of this point.

At the heart of sense experience, the analogy between painting and language is perfect. One consists of the combination of a limited series of sounds; the other of the combination of a series of lines and colors. Painting obeys the same rules of opposition and affinity which govern language; in the one, combination produces visual forms, in the other, verbal forms. Just as the word is a repository of a gamut of approximate meanings, one of which is actualized in the phrase according to its position in context, so a color has no value in itself: it is nothing but a relation, "the accord between two tones." Thus it cannot be absolutely defined: "Colors only exist relatively." It should be added that drawing is nothing but a system of lines, a conjunction of relationships. Now, as the sphere of the senses is abandoned—in language sound, color and line in painting—a notable difference emerges: a phrase (combination of words) is translated by another phrase; a picture (combination of colors and lines) is translated by a phrase. The transition from what can be grasped by the senses to what can be understood is not accomplished in the picture but outside it: the *meaning* unfolds in a nonpictorial sphere. Or, in other words, the language of painting is a system of signs that find their meaning in other systems. Baudelaire himself says it: color is a cloak or, to use the musical analogy again, an accompaniment.

All the pictorial works of all civilizations—except the merely decorative and those of the modern period—present two levels: one properly speaking pictorial, the other extra- or metapictorial. The first is made up of the relations between colors and lines; those relations construct or, more precisely, *weave* the second level: a real or imaginary object. The pictorial level refers us to a representation, and this refers us to a world which is no longer that of the painting. Of course, all representation is symbolic and the object depicted is never just a copy or representation of the original. Another peculiarity to note: the less representative the object, the less pictorial the painting tends to be, and the more to be confused with writing. For instance, in Islamic culture the arabesque, the colors on the walls at Teotihuacán and in the Mexican codices, the tantric painting in Buddhist and Hindu India. In this last, the colors and lines think and speak for themselves because, at the border between word and painting, they are articulated as a discourse. When we contemplate a roll of tantric paintings, we do not see a succession of scenes and landscapes as in Chinese painting, but rather we read a ritual. The painting frees itself from the tyranny of representation only to fall into the servitude of writing. Thus the pictorial values are not autonomous: they always build toward the representation of a real or ideal object. Without them, there would be no representation; without it, painting would have no meaning.

The object, what presents itself to the eyes or the imagination, never appears as it is. The form in which the presence appears is the representation. Being is invisible, and we are doomed to perceive it through a veil woven of symbols. The world is a cluster of signs. Representation signifies the distance between the full presence and our gazing: it is the sign of our changing and finite being in time, the mask of death. At the same time, it is the bridge across—if not to the pure and full presence—at least to its reflection: our answer to death and to being, to the unthinkable and the unspeakable. If representation does not abolish distance—the sense of a thing never entirely coincides with its being—it is the transfiguration of presence, its metaphor.

No civilization placed in doubt the relationship between the pictorial and the metapictorial, plastic values and representation. The more or less clear awareness of that relation precluded, it seems to me, the confusion between one level and another: what was distinctive, "worth seeing," was not the theme or the object represented but the painting itself, though invariably and necessarily in relation to what it represented. Color and line constituted the representation, and it gave them meaning. But as soon as painting begins to gain autonomy, this relation becomes contradictory. Even though the process begins in the Renaissance, from the critical point of view the beginning of the break is in Kant's aesthetics: the contemplation of the beautiful lays stress on the pictorial. At the same time, modern philosophy submits traditional certainties, systems, and beliefs to a radical analysis; the old meanings disperse and the representations with them. From Baudelaire on, the relation breaks: colors and lines cease to serve representative ends and aspire to mean in themselves. Painting no longer weaves a presence: it *is* presence. This break opens a double way which is also an abyss. If color and line are really a presence, they cease to be a language and the picture reverts to the world of things. That has been the fate of much contemporary painting. The other direction, foreseen by Baudelaire, can be stated in the formula: Color thinks, painting is a language. It is the other route of modern art, the way of catharsis.

In renouncing the representation that gave it meaning, painting becomes a clutch of signs projected on a space void of meanings. The old space where representation lived is deserted, or rather covered with riddles: what does the painting say? The relation between the spectator and the work suffers a radical inversion: the work is no longer the answer to the spectator's question but itself becomes a question. The answer (that is, the meaning) depends on who is looking at the picture. Painting suggests contemplation to us—not of what it shows but of a presence which the colors and forms evoke without ever entirely revealing: a presence that is in fact invisible. Painting is a language which cannot say, except by omission and allusion: the picture presents us with the signs of an absence.

The first consequence of the break was the substitution of literal for analogical interpretation, the end of criticism as judgment and the birth of poetic criticism. No less decisive was the masking of presence. Earlier painting not only alluded to a presence but, as it represented it, wove a transparency: not the embodiment of presence but its transfiguration. If representation gave meaning to painting, painting gave life to meaning: it filled it with life. By giving it form, it transformed it into a visible, palpable image. From Baudelaire on, painting thinks but does not speak, is language but does not mean; it is luminous matter and form, but it has ceased to be image. Baudelaire is original not only because he was among the first to formulate an aesthetic of modern art; it must also be said that he suggested to us an aesthetic of disembodiment.

All Baudelaire's critical writing is pervaded by a contradictory tension. The opposition between the pictorial and the metapictorial, in the end resolved to the advantage of the former, is reproduced too in the contradictory relationship between "the eternal and the ephemeral": the ideal model and the unique beauty. As in the case of color, the eternal and the ephemeral refuse to be defined separately. The eternal is what cannot be defined by the substitution of an epithet, what serves as the ground against which the modern stands out clearly. Baudelaire's descriptions are negative and tend to underline the static and undifferentiated character both of the eternal and of the classical ideal of beauty. By contrast, the modern and its equivalent in space—the unique and the bizarre—are dynamic and positive. They are the break— a break which ensures continuity; they are innovation—an innovation which reintroduces in the present an immemorial principle. Baudelaire's attitude once again implies an inversion of the traditional perspective. Before, the past, taken to be the repository of the eternal, defined the present; and it defined it strictly: artistic creation was an imitation of archetypes, whether these were works of antiquity or of nature itself. Now the eternal depends upon the present: on the one hand, the present is the criticism of tradition, so that each moment is, at the same time, a refutation of eternity and its metamorphosis into an ephemeral novelty; on the other hand, the eternal is not single but manifold and there are as many beauties as there are races, ages, and civilizations: "Every people is academic in its judgment of others, barbarous when others judge it." Recovery of the art of non-European peoples: "The beautiful is always the bizarre." But what is the bizarre? Again, it is nothing except a relationship.

It is not hard to understand why Baudelaire was reluctant to face definition: it is impossible to construct a system founded upon the value of the ephemeral and the particular because both are, by their very nature, what escapes definition, the unknown quantity which dissolves systems. Precisely because, though always present, the modern and the bizarre are unpredictable and changing realities, every system is unreal, even those which claim to be established on an eternal precept. The system is "a kind of condemnation which forces us into a perpetual recantation. . . . To elude the horror of those philosophical apostasies, I have resigned myself proudly to modesty: I am content to feel." An aesthetic which renounces reflection, an art without a head? Rather, an aesthetic which inclines toward the horrors and marvels of succession, an art fascinated by the renewed appearance of the sign of death in every living form.

Given that the modern cannot be defined, Baudelaire gives us a list of contrasts. The antique is characterized by public ostentation; the modern by private life. In one, hierarchy and ceremony; in the other, democracy and simplicity. By their cut and color, antique clothes make life a spectacle and exalt whoever wears them; modern clothes, black or dark of hue, are the expression of universal equality and serve not to expose but to conceal. Antique fashion separates, points up, distinguishes; the modern is "an identical livery of desolation . . . an immense procession of grave-diggers, political grave-diggers, lover grave-diggers, bourgeois grave-diggers. We all celebrate a burial." Here once more the law of contrast or complementary opposition intervenes: in a uniformed society, those who concentrate in themselves a uniqueness are not representative individuals, as in ancient times, but eccentrics and marginal people: the dandy, the artist, criminals, harlots, the lonely man lost in the crowd, the beggar, the wanderer. Not the men of note, exceptional men. Modern beauty is strangeness. But then, what would Baudelaire have said if confronted with the socialization of dandyism in Carnaby Street? Our modernity is the opposite of his: we have turned eccentricity into a vulgar consumer value. Three moments in Western civilization: in the ancien régime, private life lived as ceremony; in the nineteenth century, lived as in a secret novel; in the twentieth century, private life lived publicly.

For Baudelaire, the modern is the opposite of publicity; it is the unusual, so long as it is private and even secret. Thus the importance of makeup and masks which at the same time reveal and conceal. In women, the modern is the "secret distinction," a kind of "infernal or divine heroism": the bedroom as a cave of witchcraft or the sanctuary of a bloody priestess. Also modern are "humor," melancholy, disdain, the desolated sensibility, synesthesia, spirituality, a taste for infinities, fantasy, the voyage—not to conquer territories but to flee the world of progress. In short: subjectivity, subjective beauty. Composed of opposites, the modern is also the reality of the street, the motley crowd, and fashions. There is an antique death and a modern one. Hercules commits suicide because "the burns from his tunic were unbearable," Cato because "he can do nothing more for liberty," and Cleopatra because "she loses her throne and her lover . . . but none of them destroys himself in order to change his skin in view of metempsychosis," as Balzac's hero does. What then is the modern if not the appetite for change—and more: the *consciousness* of change? The ancients had an idea of the past from which they judged the changes of the present; the moderns have an idea of change and from it they judge the past and the present. That consciousness has another name: *misfortune*. It is the mark which the elect wear on their brow, and in it the bizarre, the irregular, and the deformed, all those attributes of modern beauty, are summarized. The sign of the modern is a stigma: presence wounded by time, tattooed by death.

In ancient times, men could not escape eternity, whether pagan destiny or Christian providence; modern man is condemned to the present, to instability. There is no repose. It doesn't matter: there is an instant in which time, which cannot be restrained, turns on itself; an instant not outside time but before history and the *reverse* of the present. It is the original instant, and in it modernity discovers itself as antiquity without dates: the time of the savage. When it destroys the idea of eternal beauty, the modern opens the doors to the world of savages: the most modern art is thus the most ancient. Thence the greatness of Delacroix:

his painting is "cannibal painting." With a kind of rabid enthusiasm, Baudelaire exalts the painter's "savagery," his affinity with the Aztec priest with his obsidian knife, the destructive "Molochlike" character of his work, like the "triumphal hymns" of fire. Delacroix's stains of color excite in the spirit the ferocity of certain tropical twilights, the density of the hot ash on the ruins. The original instant does not detain time: it is the other face of the present, just as barbarism is the other side of civilization. Prisoners of relation, one depends on the other: the savage is so only from the civilized perspective. Moreover, as Baudelaire's successors were not slow to prove, "savagery" is no less diverse than "the modern": there are as many artistic styles as there are primitive societies. Savagery is another illusion of modernity. At the same time, it is a criticism of modernity. Savagery, modernity, and tradition are manifestations of the art of criticism, that is to say, of polemical and historical art. When he introduces the notions of modernity and savagery into art, Baudelaire inserts criticism into the creation, invents critical art. Previously criticism preceded or followed creation; now it goes hand in hand with it and is, he would say, its condition. Just as criticism becomes a creation by analogy, so creation is also criticism because it is historical. In constant battle with the past, modern art is in conflict with itself. The art of our time lives and dies of modernity.

BOTH FROM THE PERSPECTIVE OF LANGUAGE and from that of history, Baudelaire's reflection opens out into an unsustainable paradox which is, nonetheless, the very reality of modern painting: the triumph of the pictorial is the equivalent of the disembodiment of presence, the victory of modernity is its ruin, the original moment does not dissolve but affirms history, the aesthetic of particularity refutes itself, and the creative accident turns into a mechanical repetition. Torn between these antithetical contraries, Baudelaire seeks in analogy a system which, without suppressing tensions, resolves them into a harmony. Analogy is the highest function of the imagination, since it fuses analysis and synthesis, translation and creation. It is knowledge of and at the same time a transmutation of reality. On the one hand, it is an arch that joins different historical periods and civilizations; on the other, it is a bridge between different languages: poetry, music, painting. In the first instance, if it is not "the eternal" it is what articulates all times and all spaces in an image which, ceaselessly changing, prolongs and perpetuates itself. In the second instance, it transforms communication into creation: what painting says without telling, turns into what music paints without painting, and what—without ever expressly mentioning it—the poetic word enunciates.

This differs from the old sense of analogy in this respect: the medieval artist had a universe with signs accessible to all and governed by a single code: Scripture; the modern artist has a repertory of heterogeneous signs and, instead of sacred writings, confronts a multitude of contradictory books and traditions. Thus modern analogy also flows out into the dispersal of meaning. Analogical translation is a rotating metaphor which engenders another metaphor which in turn provokes another and another: what do all these metaphors say? Nothing that the painting has not already said: presence is concealed to the extent that the meaning is dissolved.

In many of his poems and critical reflections, Baudelaire has stated unequivocally what the *ultimate sense* of analogy is. Particularly explicit are the pages he devotes to the music of Wagner. More than a reflection on analogy, those pages tell of a unique experience which we have no choice but to call *the disembodiment of presence*. When he hears the overture to *Lohengrin*, he feels himself released from "the fetters of gravity," so that, rocked by the music, he finds himself "in a solitude with an immense horizon and a vast diffuse light; immensity with no integrity other than itself. Soon I experience the feeling of an even livelier clarity;

the intensity of the light increased so quickly that dictionary words would be inadequate to express that superabundance, end-lessly reborn, of ardor and whiteness. Then I conceived clearly the idea of a soul moving in a luminous atmosphere, an ecstasy composed of voluptuousness and knowledge. . . ." The sensations of altitude and voluptuousness are closely associated with those of the loss of body and of that white light which is the abolition of all color. Empty of itself, his being rests in an immensity which contains nothing but itself. Again and again the notion of time is changed into that of space which extends "to the remotest conceivable limits." The feeling of being at a frontier: space extends so far that in fact it is invisible and inconceivable: non-space, non-time. The ecstasy of knowledge consists in this annulment: immersed in the floating space, the poet becomes detached from his identity and fused with vacant extension. The critical art culminates in a final negation: Baudelaire contem-plates, literally, *nothing*. Or rather, he contemplates a metaphor of nothingness. A transparency that, if it hides nothing, reflects nothing either—not even his questioning face. The aesthetic of analogy is the aesthetic of the annihilation of presence.

BAUDELAIRE'S THOUGHT gave a critical and aesthetic con-science to almost all the artistic movements of our time, from impressionism to the present. The idea of painting as an auton-omous and self-sufficient language has been shared by the ma-jority of artists of our time and was the foundation of abstract painting. A little more should be said about the value, at once polemical and magical, of the word *modernity* and of its descen-dants: the new, the avant-garde (though Baudelaire does not conceal his revulsion for this term). It is worth bearing in mind that a constant note in modern art has been the use of procedures and styles each time more remote from Renaissance and Greco-Roman traditions, everything from black art to pre-Columbian art, from the painting of children to that of schizophrenics; plurality of the ideas of beauty. The preeminence of spontaneity, the communication between waking and dream, the nostalgia for a word lost in the beginnings of time, and the exaltation of childhood are themes which reappear in impressionism, surrealism, and abstract expressionism. The reduction of beauty to the singular, the characteristic, or the monstrous: expressionism. The creative function of analogy, the aesthetic of surprise: Breton, Apollinaire.

In a sense, it could be said that modern art has fulfilled Baudelaire. It would also be right to say that it has contradicted him. These two statements are not mutually exclusive but complementary: the situation in 1967 is as much the negation of that of 1860 as its result. In recent decades the acceleration of changes has been such that it almost amounts to a refutation of change: immobility and repetition. The same happens with the increasing production of more and more works, each one pretending to be exceptional and unique: apart from the fact that most are the daughters of industrious imitation and not of imagination, they give us the impression of a huge heaping-up of heteroclite objects—the confusion of refuse. Marcel Duchamp asks himself: "We are drowned in a sea of paintings . . . where are the granaries and cellars which could contain them?" Modernity ends by negating itself: the vanguard of 1967 repeats the achievements and gestures of the 1917 vanguard. We are living through the end of the idea of modern art. Thus the first thing artists and critics would have to do would be to apply to that idea the rigorous criticism that Baudelaire applied to the notion of "tradition."

The aesthetics of modernity are contemporary with certain changes in the production, distribution, and evaluation of works. The autonomy of painting—its separation from the other arts and its claim to constitute itself as a self-sufficient language—is parallel to the birth of the museum, the commercial gallery, the professional critic, and the collector. It is a movement which, as we all know, begins in the Renaissance and whose peak coincides with that of capitalism and the free market. There is more to be said about the evolution of the forms of artistic production, from the workshops of the Renaissance and the baroque period to the individual producer of our time. But what I want to highlight is a double phenomenon: on the one hand, paintings ceased to belong to a system of common meanings and beliefs and became instead more and more individual, intended to satisfy consumers who were also individuals; on the other, wrenched out of the old collective space, temple or palace, they constituted for themselves an autonomous space. In the spiritual and social quite as much as in the material sense, paintings became movables. This circumstance facilitated their introduction into the marketplace.

Ambivalence of the painting: it is art, a unique object; it is merchandise, something we can shift about and hang on this wall or that. Nothing more natural than that a society which adores things and has made financial transaction the highest form of communication should build museums and multiply private collections: they are the counterpart of banks and stores. The fetishism of things is different from the idolatry of images. The first is the passion of an owner enslaved by what he possesses, quite independent of the meaning of the object; the other is a religious passion for what the image represents. Works of art are unique but, at the same time, are interchangeable: they can be sold; idols are neither unique nor interchangeable: an image can be exchanged for another only by means of an appropriate rite. Our society exalts the painter and his works as a condition of converting them into objects of exchange.

Criticism of the aesthetics of modernity requires equally a criticism of the marketplace and of the magical-market nature of the work. Time and again artists have rebelled against this situation. Dadaism undermined the notion of the "work" and demonstrated the laughable character of the art cult; surrealism revived the image and devalued the pictorial. Even so, the "readymades" of

Duchamp and the visions of Ernst and Miró figure in the museums. In recent years, from a different perspective, other young artists struggle to escape the cage of the marketplace. Among these attempts I single out, because of the radicalism of their program, that of the *Groupe de recherche d'art visuel*. These artists have dared to put themselves in the path of the bull, as bullfight aficionados say. In other words: they attack the system and its principles. In the first place, they revert to teamwork. Baudelaire in his lifetime, faced with the spectacle of hundreds of painters in search of an impossible and in the final account an inane originality, was pointing out how much better it would have been for them had they worked honorably in the studio of a master. Painting itself would have benefited: "A vast output is nothing more than a thought with a thousand arms." The *Groupe de recherche d'art visuel* substitutes the studio for the laboratory, artisanal production for research, the idea of the master-patron for the association of artists, and sets at the center of its concerns that *thought* of which Baudelaire speaks and which is nothing but another name for imagination. An end to the superstition attached to the profession: "Who possesses only ability is a dolt." An end to the fanaticism of the unique object, as much by the multiplication of specimens of each work as by making each one of them an object which invites us to contemplate and transform it. And an end to the idea of the spectator; instead, creative interplay: the *Groupe* suggests situations which provoke a joint reaction from those who participate.

The work dissolves into life, but life is resolved in *fiesta*. This word immediately evokes one of the myths of modernity: Baudelaire's savage, Breton's "far off man." Only now it's not a matter of reverting to the art of primitive men or of reviving their beliefs, but of finding, thanks specifically to our machines, a collective way to consume and to consummate time. Le Parc has said that a painting lasts as long as a look. That is true, if the look is a sign of intelligence which we pass over the work. . . . I do not know if the works of the *Groupe* will end up in museums, as those of their predecessors have. It's a safe bet. It does not matter: I've cited the attempt by these young artists because their program seems to be a symptom, among others, of the disappearance of the "idea of modernity," as Baudelaire and his successors conceived it, from the impressionists to the abstract painters. I am sure that we are witnesses to the end of the "art object" and the conception of art as the mere production of objects. The notion of substance dissolves not only in contemporary philosophy and physics, but even in the world of economics: considerations of use displace increasingly valuation in terms of durability. I will add finally that my idea of the *fiesta* differs from that proposed by these young artists. The *fiesta* I dream of would not only be the sharing and consummation of the object, but, unlike that of the primitives, it would *have no object*: not commemoration of an anniversary nor a return to past time; it would be— I have no choice but to force language so that I can say it—the dissipation of time, *production of forgetfulness.*

The resurrection of the *fiesta* is one of the unravelings of contemporary art, as much in the domain of the visual as of the musical and verbal arts: a dissolving of the art object in the temporal current and the crystallization of historical time in a closed space. The *fiesta* suppresses, for a moment, the opposition between presence and representation, the atemporal and the historical, the sign and the object signified. It is a presentation but at the same time a consummation: presence embodies only to share itself out and to be consumed among the communicants. Thus, at one extreme, the quarrel between the eternal and the ephemeral is settled. But from the ashes of *fiesta* discord between the pictorial and the metapictorial revives. Is there another way?

Doubtfully and guided by the principle of analogy, which is also that of complementary opposition, I venture an hypothesis: the pole opposite to *fiesta* is contemplation. If the first supplies a lack in our mass society, the second satisfies another lack in our society of solitaries. The art of contemplation produces objects but it does not consider them things, rather signs: points of departure toward the discovery of another reality, whether of presence or absence. I write "toward the discovery" because in a society like ours art offers us neither meanings nor representations: it is art in search of meaning. An art in search of presence or of absence where meanings dissolve. This art of contemplation would redeem the notion of *oeuvre* except that, instead of perceiving in it an object, a thing, it would give it back its true function: of being a *bridge* between the spectator and that presence to which art always alludes without ever entirely naming.

After more than a century of modernism, our situation is rather like that of the character in *Kantan*, that No play admirably translated by Arthur Waley: a young walker finds accommodation in an inn and, tired from his journey, stretches out on a mat; while the innkeeper prepares him a handful of rice, he dreams that he accedes to the throne of China and that he lives, as though he were immortal, fifty years of glory: the few minutes it took for the rice to cook and for him to wake up. Like the Buddhist pilgrim, we can ask ourselves: has something changed? If we answer: nothing has changed because all the changes were made of the substance of the dream, we will implicitly affirm that we have changed. Before dreaming that dream we could not have answered thus; but to know that changes are chimerical, we should change. If we respond in the affirmative, we will incur a contradiction, too: our change consists in perceiving that all changes are illusory, our own being no exception. The art and criticism of the twentieth century have been prisoners of this paradox. Perhaps the only answer is not to ask the question, to get up and wander on in search of presence, not as if nothing had happened but as if everything had—that everything which is identical with nothing.

Delhi, December 1967

65

ANDRÉ BRETON,
OR THE SEARCH FOR
THE BEGINNING

It is not possible to write about André Breton with unimpassioned language. What's more, it would be wrong to do so. For him, the powers of the word were indistinguishable from those of passion, and this, in its highest and tensest form, was nothing but language in a state of savage purity: poetry. Breton: the language of passion—the passion of language. His whole research, quite as much as—if not more than—an exploration of unknown psychic territories, was the repossession of a lost kingdom: the word of the beginning, man before men and civilizations. Surrealism was an order of chivalry and its whole enterprise was a *quête du graal*. The surprising evolution of the Spanish term *querer* expresses well the tone of the search: *querer* comes from *quaerere* (to seek, to inquire), but in Spanish it soon changed its meaning to signify impassioned will, desire. *Querer*: passional, amorous search. Search not toward the future or the past but toward that center of convergence which is, simultaneously, the origin and end of time: the day before the beginning and after the end. His outrage at "the infamous Christian idea of sin" is something more than a rejection of traditional Western values: it is an affirmation of man's original innocence. This distinguishes him from almost all his contemporaries and from those who followed him. For Bataille, eroticism, death, and sin are interchangeable signs which repeat in their combinations, with terrifying monotony, the same meaning: the nothingness of man, his irremediable abjection. For Sartre, too, man is the son of a curse, either ontological or historical, call it anxiety or salaried work. Both are rebel sons of Christianity. The origin of Breton is other. In his life and work he was not so much the heir of Sade and Freud as of Rousseau and Eckhart. He was not a philosopher but a poet and, what is more, in the old sense of the term, a man of honor. His intransigence on the idea of sin was a point of honor: it seemed to him that sin was, in effect, a *stain*, something which wounded not human *being* but human dignity. Belief in sin was incompatible with his notion of man. This conviction, which set him very violently against many modern philosophies and all religions, was at its root religious too: it was an act of faith. What is most strange—I should say admirable—is that he never abandoned that faith. He denounced frailties, faintings, and treacheries, but he never thought our guilt congenital. He was a party man without the least trace of Manichaeism. For Breton, sin and birth were not synonymous.

Man, even when degraded by the neocapitalism and pseudo-socialism of our times, is a marvelous being because, sometimes, he *speaks*. Language is the mark, or the sign, not of his fall but of his essential irresponsibility. By means of the word we can accede to the lost kingdom and recover old powers. Those powers are not ours. The inspired man, the one who speaks in truth, says nothing that is his: language speaks through his mouth.

Dream lends itself to the explosion of the word because it is an affective state: its passivity is the activity of desire. Dream is passionate. Here too his opposition to Christianity was religious in character: language, to speak to itself, annihilates conscience. Poetry does not save the "I" of the poet, it dissolves it in the vaster and more powerful reality of speech. The practice of poetry requires abandonment, renunciation of the "I." It is sad that Buddhism did not interest him: that tradition too destroys the illusion of the "I," though not for the benefit of language but of silence. (I should add that that silence is a quietened word, a silence which does not cease to emit meanings from more than two thousand years ago.) I am reminded of Buddhism because I believe that "automatic writing" is rather like a modern equivalent of Buddhist meditation; I do not think it is a method for writing poems, nor is it a rhetorical recipe: it is a psychic exercise, a convocation and an invocation destined to open the floodgates of verbal flow. Poetic automatism, as Breton himself stressed many times, is a neighbor of asceticism: it implies a state of difficult passivity which, in turn, requires the abolition of all criticism and self-criticism. It is a radical criticism of criticism, a placing of conscience under interdict. In its fashion, it is a way of purgation, a means of negation which tends to provoke the appearance of true reality: primordial language.

The basis of "automatic writing" is a belief in the identity between speaking and thinking. Man does not speak because he thinks but thinks because he speaks; or rather, speaking is not distinct from thought: to speak is to think. Breton justifies this idea with his observation: "Nous ne disposons spontanément pour nous exprimer que d'une *seule* structure verbale excluant de la manière la plus catégorique toute autre structure apparemment chargée du même sens." The first objection which could be raised against this cutting formula is the fact that both in daily speech and in written prose we are confronted with phrases which could be said in other words or with the same words in a different order. Breton could answer, rightly, that between one version and another not only does the syntactical structure change but the idea itself is modified, however imperceptibly. Every change in the verbal structure produces a change of meaning. In a strict sense, what we call synonyms are nothing but translations or equivalences within a language; and what we call translation is transfer or interpretation. Words such as *nirvana, dharma, tao*, or *jen* are in fact untranslatable; the same happens with *physics, nature, democracy, revolution*, and other Western terms which have no exact equivalent in languages alien to our tradition. The more intimate the relation between the verbal structure and the meaning—mathematics and poetry, to avoid talking of unarticulated languages such as music and painting—the more difficult translation becomes. At either extreme of language—exclamation and equation—it is impossible to separate the sign from its two halves: signifier and signified are the same. Breton thus opposes, perhaps without knowing it, Saussure: language is not only an arbitrary convention between sound and sense, something the linguists themselves are now coming to recognize.

Breton's ideas about language were magical in nature. Not only did he refrain from distinguishing magic and poetry, but he always thought that the latter was effectively a force, a substance or an energy capable of changing reality. At the same time, those ideas had a precision and penetration which I dare to call scientific. On the one hand, he saw language as an autonomous current endowed with its own power, a kind of universal magnetism; on the other, he conceived that erotic substance as a system of signs ruled by a double law of affinity and opposition, similarity and otherness. This vision is not far from that of the modern linguists: words and their constituent elements are fields of energy, like atoms and their particles. The attraction between syllables and words is not different from that of stars and bodies. The ancient notion of analogy reappears: nature is language, and language, for its part, is a double of nature. To recover natural language is to return to nature, before the fall and before history: poetry is the witness of original innocence. The *Social Contract* becomes, for Breton, a verbal, a poetic accord between man and nature, word and thought. From this perspective one can better understand that often repeated assertion: Surrealism is a movement of total liberation, not a poetic school. Poetry, the route to reconquering innocent language and renewing the original contract, is the scripture of the foundation of man. Surrealism is revolutionary because it is a return to the origin of the origin.

The earliest poems of Breton reveal the traces of an impassioned reading of Mallarmé. Not even at the moments of greatest verbal violence and freedom did he abandon that taste for the word, at once precise and precious. Iridescent word, language of reverberations. He was a "mannerist" poet in the good sense of the term; within the European tradition he belongs to that strain which descends from Góngora, Marino, Donne—poets whose work I do not know if he read and who, I fear, his poetic morality reproved. Verbal splendor, and violence of mind and passion. A strange alliance, but not all that uncommon, between prophecy and aestheticism which makes his best poems into objects of beauty and, at the same time, into spiritual testaments. That is, perhaps, the reason for his cult of Lautréamont, the poet who found the *form* of psychic explosion. Thence, too, his avowed repugnance for the simplistic brutality of Dada, though he judged it inevitable and welcome as a "revolutionary necessity." His reservations about other poets are different in nature. His admiration of Apollinaire contains a grain of reticence because for Breton poetry was the creation of reality by means of the word and not just verbal inventiveness. He loved novelty and surprise in art, but the term *invention* was not to his liking; on the other hand, in many of his texts the noun *revelation* glows with an unequivocal light. Saying is the highest form of activity: to reveal what is hidden, to waken the buried word, to provoke the emergence of our double, to create that other which we are and which we never entirely cease to be.

Revelation is resurrection, exposure, initiation. It is a word that evokes rite and ceremony. Except as a means of provocation, to outrage the public or incite rebellion, Breton despised open-air spectacles. The fiesta should be celebrated in the catacombs. Each of the surrealist exhibitions revolved around a contradictory axis: scandal and secret, consecration and profanation. Consecration and conspiracy are kindred terms; revelation is also rebellion. The *other*, our double, denies the illusory coherence and security of our conscience, that pillar of smoke which supports our arrogant philosophical and religious constructions. The *others*, proletarians and colonial slaves, primitive myths and revolutionary utopias, threaten with no less violence the beliefs and institutions of the West. Breton extends his hand to both, to Fourier and to the Papuas from New Guinea. Rebellion and revelation, language and passion, are manifestations of a single reality. The true name of that reality is also double: innocence and marvel. Man is creator of marvels, is a poet, because he is an innocent being. Children, women, lovers, those inspired and even the mad are the embodiment of the marvelous. All they do is unexpected and unpremeditated. They don't know what they do: they're irresponsible, innocent. Magnets, lightning rods, high-power cables: their words and deeds are nonsensical and yet have a meaning. They are the scattered signs of a language in constant movement which spreads before our eyes a fan of contradictory meanings—resolved at last in a unique and ultimate sense. Through them and in them the universe talks to us and to itself.

I've repeated some of his words: revelation and rebellion, innocence and marvel, passion and language. There is another: magnetism. Breton was one of the centers of gravity of our age. Not only did he believe that men are governed by the laws of attraction and repulsion but that his person was itself an embodiment of those forces. All of us who had anything to do with him experienced that dual, dizzying feeling: fascination and the centrifugal impulse. I confess that for a long time I was kept awake by the worry that I might do or say something to provoke his reproof. I believe many of his friends had a similar experience. Just a few years ago Buñuel invited me to view, in private, one of his films. When it was over, he asked me: "Will Breton find it to be in the surrealist tradition?" I cite Buñuel not only as a great artist, but because he is a man of really exceptional integrity of character and freedom of spirit. These feelings, experienced by all those who visited Breton regularly, had nothing to do with fear of or respect for a superior (though I believe that, if there are superior men, Breton was one of them). I never saw him as a chief, still less as a Pope, to use the ignoble term popularized by certain fools. Despite my friendship with him personally, my activities with the surrealist group were tangential. Still, his affection and generosity always confused me, from the beginning of our relationship to the end of his days. I have never known why he put up with me: perhaps because I was from Mexico, a country he always loved? Beyond these private considerations, I should say that I write as if I were engaged in silent dialogue with Breton: reply, answer, coincidence, disagreement, homage, all together. Even as I write now I experience that feeling.

In my adolescence, during a period of isolation and exaltation, I read by chance some pages which, I learned later, form chapters of L'amour fou. In them Breton describes his climb to the summit of the Teides, in Tenerife. That text, read at almost the same time as Blake's The Marriage of Heaven and Hell, opened the doors of modern poetry to me. It was an "art of love," not in the trivial way of Ovid's, but as an initiation into something which later life and my experience of the Orient have confirmed: the analogy, or better said, the identity between woman and nature. Is the water feminine or is woman a surge of waves, a nocturnal river, a dawn beach tattooed by the wind? If we are a metaphor of the universe, the human couple is the metaphor par excellence, the point in which all forces meet, the seed of all forms. The couple is, again, reconquered time, time before time. Against wind and tide, I have tried to be true to that revelation; the word *love* preserves intact all its powers over me. Or as he says, "On n'en sera plus jamais quitte avec ces frondaisons de l'age d'or." In all his writing, first to last, this obstinate belief in a paradisiac age appears, joined to the vision of the primordial couple. Woman is bridge, place of reconciliation between the natural and human world. She is solid language, embodied revelation: "Le femme n'est plus qu'un calice débordante de voyelles."

Years later I got to know Benjamin Péret, Leonora Carrington, Wolfgang Paalen, Remedios Varo, and other surrealists who had sought refuge in Mexico during the Second World War. Peace came and I saw Benjamin again in Paris. He took me to the café at Place Blanche. For a long time I saw Breton regularly. Though regular contact is not always beneficial to the exchange of ideas and feelings, more than once I felt that current which really joins speakers together, even if their points of view are not identical. I shall never forget, among all those conversations, one which we had in the summer of 1964, shortly before I was to return to India. I remember it not because it was the last but because of the atmosphere that surrounded it. This is not the occasion to recount that episode (one day, I promise myself, I will). For me it was an *encounter*, in the sense which Breton gave the word: predestination and, at the same time, election. That night, as we walked alone together through the neighborhood of Les Halles, the conversation veered toward a theme which preoccupied him: the future of the surrealist movement. I remember saying to him, roughly, that for me surrealism was the sacred illness of our world, like leprosy in the Middle Ages or the Spanish "illuminati" of the sixteenth century; a necessary negation of the West, it would live much as modern civilization did, independent of political systems and the ideologies that would predominate in the future. My exaltation impressed him, but he replied, "Negation lives as a function of affirmation and vice versa; I very much doubt that the world beginning now can be defined as affirmation or negation: we come into a neutral zone and the surrealist rebellion should express itself in forms which are neither negation nor affirmation. . . ." It is not outrageous to suggest that this idea inspired the last exhibition of the group: absolute separation. This is not the first time Breton asked for the "concealment" of surrealism, but he seldom declared his wish so decisively. Perhaps he thought the movement would recover its fertility only if it demonstrated its ability to change itself into an underground force. Return to the catacombs? I don't know. I asked myself if in a society like ours, in which the old contradictions have vanished—not to the benefit of the principle of identity but by a kind of universal annulment and devaluation—what Mallarmé called "restricted action" still has meaning: is publishing still a form of action, or is it a way of dissolving it in the anonymity of publicity?

It is often said that the ambiguity of surrealism consists of the fact that it was a movement of poets and painters which, nonetheless, refuses to be judged by aesthetic criteria. Is this not the case with all past artistic trends and with all the works of the great poets and painters? "Art" is an invention of aesthetics, which, in turn, is an invention of philosophers. Nietzsche buried both and danced on their tomb: what we call art is a game. The surrealist desire to erase the borders between art and life is not new; what are new are the terms in which it expressed itself, and new also is the meaning of its action. Neither "artistic life" nor "vital art": to return to the word's origin, to the moment at which speaking is synonymous with creating. I do not know what future there is for the surrealist group; I am sure that the current which runs from German romanticism and from Blake to surrealism will not disappear. It will live at the margin. It will be the *other* voice.

Surrealism, critics say, is no longer the vanguard. Besides the fact that I dislike that military term, I do not believe that novelty, that being on the point of happening, is an essential characteristic of surrealism. Not even Dada had that frenetic cult of the new which the futurists, for example, postulated. Neither Dada nor surrealism worships machines. Surrealism profaned them: unproductive machines, "élevages de poussière," melting watches. The machine as a method of criticism of the worship of machine and of men who worship progress and its farces. Is Duchamp the beginning or the end of painting? By his oeuvre and even more by his attitude which denied the oeuvre, Duchamp concludes a period of Western art (that of painting properly speaking) and opens another which is no longer "artistic": the dissolution of art in life, language in the closed circle of the game of words, reason in its philosophical antidote—laughter. Duchamp dissolves the modern with the same gesture he uses to deny tradition. In the case of Breton, moreover, there is the vision of time not as a succession but as the constant, though invisible, presence of an innocent present. The future struck him as fascinating because it was the territory of the unexpected: not what will be according to reason, but what might be according to imagination. The destruction of the actual world would permit the appearance of real time, not historical but natural, not ruled by progress but by desire. This, if I have it right, was his idea of a Communist-libertarian society. He never thought that there was an essential contradiction between myths and utopias, poetry and revolutionary programs. He read Fourier as we can read the Vedas or the Popol Vuh, and the Eskimos' poems struck him as revolutionary prophecies. The most ancient past and the furthest future came together naturally in his spirit. Similarly: his materialism was not a vulgar "scientism," nor was his irrationality a hatred of reason.

The decision to embrace opposite terms—Sade and Rousseau, Novalis and Roussel, Juliette and Eloise, Marx and Chateaubriand—appears constantly in his writings and in his actions.

Nothing is further removed from this attitude than the complacent tolerance of skepticism. In the world of thought he hated eclecticism, and in the world of eroticism he hated promiscuity. The best parts of his work—prose as well as verse—are those pages inspired by the idea of election and the correlative of fidelity to that election, whether in art or in politics, in friendship or in love. This idea was the axis of his life and the center of his conception of the single love: the luminosity of passion cut by liberty, an unalterable diamond. Our age has freed love from the prisons of the last century only to turn it into an anonymous pastime, one more consumer item in a society of extremely busy consumers. Breton's vision is the denial of almost everything which passes today for love and even for eroticism (another word carelessly handled like the paltriest coin). It is hard to understand completely his unreserved attachment to the work of Sade. True, he was moved and exalted by the absolute character of Sade's negation, but how to reconcile this with the belief in love, center of the golden age? Sade denounces love: it is a hypocrisy or, worse still, an illusion. His system is raving, not incoherent: his denial is no less complete than the affirmation of Saint Augustine. Both repudiate with identical violence all Manichaeism; for the Christian saint evil has no ontological reality; for Sade what lacks reality is what we call the good: his version of the *Social Contract* is the statutes of the Society of the Friends of Crime.

Bataille tried to turn Sade's monologue into a dialogue and set against absolute eroticism a no less absolute interlocutor: the Christian God. The result was silence and laughter: "atheology." The unthinkable and the unnameable. Breton set out to reintroduce love into eroticism or, more precisely, to consecrate eroticism by love. Again: his opposition to all religions implies a will to consecrate. And more, a will to reconcile. Commenting on a passage of the *Nouvelle Justine*—the episode in which one of the characters mixes his sperm with Etna lava—Breton observes that the act is a love homage to nature, "une façon, des plus folles, des plus indiscutables de l'aimer." True, his admiration for Sade was almost boundless and he always thought that "tant qu'on ne sera pas quitte avec l'idée de la transcendance d'un bien quelconque . . . la représentation exaltée du mal inné gardera la plus grande valeur révolutionnaire." With this reservation, in the dialogue between Sade and Rousseau, he inclines irresistibly to the latter, the friend of primitive man, the lover of nature. Love is not an illusion: it is the mediation between man and nature, the place in which earthly and spiritual magnetism cross.

Each facet of his work reflects the others. It is not the passive reflection of the mirror: it is not a repetition but a reply. Contrary beams of light, a dialogue of luminosities. Magnetism, revelation, thirst, and innocence and, at the same time, disdain. Haughty? Yes, in the noble sense of the word: a bird of prey, a bird of the heights. All the words of this family—haughty, high—suit him. He was raised up, exalted, his poetry exalts us, and, above all, he said that the bodies of woman and man were our only altars. And death? Each man is born and dies at various times. It is not the first time that Breton dies. He knew it better than anyone: each of his central books is the story of a resurrection. I know that it is different now and that we will not see him again. This death is no illusion. All the same, Breton lived certain moments, saw certain evidences which are the negation of time and of what we call a normal perspective on time. I call those instants poetic, though they are experiences common to all men: the only difference is that the poet remembers them and tries to embody them in words, sounds, colors. Whoever has lived those moments and is able to bend to their meaning knows that the "I" does not save itself because it does not exist. He knows too that, as Breton himself often stressed, the borders between dream and waking, life and death, time and timeless presence, are fluid and indecisive. We do not know what it really is to die, except that it is the end of the "I"—the end of prison. Breton broke that prison various times, enlarged or denied time, and, for an unmeasured moment, coincided with the *other* time. This experience, nucleus of his life and of his thought, is invulnerable and untouchable: it is beyond time, beyond death—beyond us. Knowing this reconciles me to his recent death and to all death.

Alternating Current, 1967

HENRI MICHAUX

I

In recent years Henri Michaux has published three books in which he tells of his encounters with mescaline (*Misérable miracle* [1956]; *L'infini turbulent* [1957]; *Paix dans les brisements* [1959]). To this must be added a disturbing series of drawings—the majority in black and white, others in color—carried out shortly after each experience. Prose, poems, and drawings interpenetrate, extend, and illuminate one another. The drawings do not merely illustrate the texts. Michaux's painting has never been subsidiary to his poetry: it is a case of worlds that are at once autonomous and complementary. But in the case of the mescaline experience the lines and the words form an entity that is difficult to separate. Shapes, ideas, and sensations tangle about each other as though they were a single, dizzying creature. In a sense the drawings, far from being *illustrations* of the written word, are a kind of *com-*

mentary. The rhythm and movement of the lines make one think of an unusual musical notation, except that we are faced not with a notation of sounds or ideas but of vertigos, lacerations, and regatherings of being. Incisions in the cortex of time, halfway between the ideographic sign and the magic inscription, characters and shapes "more perceptible than legible," these drawings are a critique of poetic and pictorial writing, that is, an extension of the sign and the image, something beyond word and line.

Painting and poetry are languages with which Michaux has striven to say something specifically unsayable. A poet, he began to paint when he perceived that this new medium would allow him to say what his poetry could no longer say. But is it a matter of saying? Perhaps Michaux has never set out to say. All of his attempts are directed at touching that zone, by definition inexpressible and unshareable, in which meanings vanish. A center null and replete, empty and full of itself at the same time. The sign and the signified—the distance between the object and the consciousness that contemplates it—evaporate in the overwhelming presence which alone exists. The work of Michaux—poems, real and imaginary journeys, paintings—is a long and sinuous expedition in the direction of some of our infinities—the most secret, the most fearful, and, at the same time, the most laughable—always in search of the *other* infinity.

Michaux travels in his languages: lines, words, colors, silences, rhythms. And he is not afraid to break the backbone of a word as the horseman who does not hesitate to wind a mount. To get—where? To that nowhere which is everywhere and here. Language-vehicle but also language-knife and miner's lamp. Language-cauterizer and language-bandage, language-fog and siren in the fog. Pickax against rock and lightning in the depths of night. Words become tools. Once more, extensions of the hand, the eye, thought. Nonartistic language. Cutting and severing words, reduced to their most immediate and aggressive function: opening a way for themselves. Yet it is a matter of paradoxical utility, since they are no longer at the service of communication but of the inexpressible. A nonhuman and maybe a superhuman enterprise. The extraordinary tension of Michaux's language is due to the fact that all his honed efficiency is governed by a will hurled into the encounter with something which is inefficient par excellence: that state of not knowing what absolute knowledge is, the thought which no longer thinks because it has merged with itself, the infinite transparency, the unmoving whirlwind.

Misérable miracle opens with these words: "This is an exploration. By means of the word, the sign, the drawing. Mescaline is what is explored." When I finished the book I asked myself if the result of the experience hadn't been the opposite: the poet Michaux explored by mescaline. Exploration or encounter? More the latter. Hand to hand with the drug, with the tremor of the earth, with the tremor of the being shaken by his inner foe—a foe that fuses itself with our own being, a foe indistinguishable and inseparable from us. Encounter with mescaline: encounter with ourselves, with the known-unknown. The double who wears our own face for a mask. The face which erases and transforms itself into an enormous mocking grin. The devil. The clown. That's not me. That is me. Martyrissible apparition. And when the face turns, there is no one. I too have left myself. Space, space, pure vibration. Great gift, present of the gods, mescaline is a window where the gaze slips away infinitely without finding anything but itself gazing. There is no I: there is a space, vibration, perpetual liveliness. Struggles, terrors, exaltations, panics, delights: is it Michaux or mescaline? It was all there in his earlier books. Mescaline was a *confirmation*. Mescaline: witness. The poet saw his inner space in the space outside. Transit from inner to outer—an outside which is interiority itself, the nucleus of reality. Atrocious, unspeakable spectacle. Michaux can say: I stepped out of my life to glimpse life.

It all begins with a vibration. Imperceptible movement which minute by minute gains momentum. Wind, a long whistling, whetted hurricane, torrent of faces, shapes, lines. Everything falling, advancing, climbing, vanishing, reappearing. Dizzying evaporation and condensation. Bubbles, bubbles, cobblestones, gravel. Stones of gas. Lines that intersect, rivers that join, infinite bifurcations, meanderings, deltas, deserts that advance, deserts that fly. Scatterings, agglutinations, fragmentations, re-formings. Broken words, coupling of syllables, fornication of meanings. Destruction of language. Mescaline rules by silence—and screams, screams without a mouth and we fall into its silence! Return to the vibrations, entry into undulations. Repetitions: mescaline is a "mechanism of the infinite." Heterogeneity, continual welling up of fragments, particles, pieces. Exasperated series. Nothing is fixed. Avalanches, rule of the uncountable number, execrable proliferation. Gangrened space, cancerous time. Is there no center? Shaken by the blast of mescaline, sucked at by the abstract whirlwind, the modern Westerner finds nothing to grasp. He has forgotten the names, God is no longer called God. For the Aztec and the Tarahumara Indian it was enough to pronounce the name for the divine presence to come down, in its infinite manifestations. Unity and plurality of the ancients. For us, lacking gods: Pullulation and Time. We have lost the names. We are left with "causes and effects, antecedents and consequences." Space full of insignificances. Heterogeneity is repetition, amorphous mass. Miserable miracle.

The first encounter with mescaline ends with the discovery of a "mechanism of the infinite." The infinite production of colors, rhythms, and forms reveals itself to be in the end a terrifying and laughable cascade of trifles. We are fairground millionaires. The second series of experiences (*L'infini turbulent*) occasioned unexpected reactions and visions. Exposed to continuous physiological discharges and to an implacable psychic tension, being opened up. The exploration of mescaline, like a fire or an earthquake, was devastating; only the essential remained standing, what was, because infinitely frail, infinitely strong. What is this power called? Is it a faculty, a power, or, better said, an absence of power, the total helplessness of man? I think it is the last. That helplessness is our strength. At the final moment, when nothing remains in us—loss of the I, loss of identity—the fusion occurs with something alien which is, nonetheless, our own, the only thing that is truly ours. The hollow, the hole which we are in, is filled to overflowing, until it becomes a fountain. In the extreme drought water springs. Perhaps there is a point of union between man's being and that of the universe. For the rest, nothing positive: hole, abyss, turbulent infinity. State of abandonment, alienation—but not madness. Madmen are locked in their madness, which is, so to speak, an ontological mistake: taking the part for the whole. Equidistant from sanity and madness, the vision Michaux tells of is total: contemplation of the demonic and the divine—there is no alternative to those terms—as an inseparable reality, as the ultimate reality. Of man or of the universe? I don't know. Perhaps of universe-man. Man penetrated, overcome by the universe.

The demonic trance was above all the revelation of a transhuman eroticism—and thus infinitely perverse. A psychic violation, an insidious opening and extending and unfolding of the most secret parts of being. Nothing sexual. An infinitely sensual universe from which the human body and form had vanished. Not the "triumph of matter" or of flesh but the vision of the other side of the spirit. Abstract lust: "Dissolution—the right word which I understood in a flash. . . . I revel in deliquescence." Temptation, in the literal sense of the word, the sense to which all great mystics (Christians, Buddhists, Moslems) have referred. Nonetheless, I confess that I do not entirely understand this passage. Perhaps Michaux's aversion stems less from contact with Eros than from the vision of cosmic confusion, that is, from the revelation of chaos. The depths of the being laid bare, the other side of the presence, the chaos is the primordial clay, the ancient disorder and, at the same time, the universal matrix. I experienced a similar sensation, though less intense, which affected only the most superficial areas of my consciousness, in the huge summer of India during my first visit in 1952. Fallen into the great panting mouth, the universe seemed to me an immense, multiple fornication. I glimpsed then the meaning of the architecture of Konarak and of ascetic eroticism. The vision of chaos is a kind of ritual bath, a regeneration by immersion in the original fountain, a genuine return to the "earlier life." Primitive men, Chinese Taoists, archaic Greeks, and other people do not fear the tremendous contact. The Western attitude is unhealthy. It is moral. Great isolator, great separator, morality splits man in two. To return to unity of vision is to reconcile body, soul, and world. At the end of the attempt Michaux recalls a fragment of a tantric poem:

> Inaccessible to impregnations,
> Enjoying all enjoyments,
> Touching all like the wind,
> Penetrated by all like the sky,
> The *yoguin* always pure
> Bathes in the perpetual river.
> Enjoys all enjoyments and nothing stains him.

The divine vision—inseparable from the demonic, since both are revelations of *unity*—began with the "apparition of the gods." Thousands, hundreds of thousands, one after another, in long queues, an infinity of august faces, horizon of beneficent presences. Astonishment and recognition. But first: sea swells of whitenesses. Everywhere whiteness, sonorous, shining. And light, seas of light. Later, the images of the gods disappeared, though the peaceful and enjoyable cascade of being did not stop welling out. Admiration: "I hold to the divine perfection of the continuance of Being throughout time, a continuance so beautiful—beautiful beyond the limits of knowledge—that the gods, as the *Mahabarata* says, the gods themselves grow jealous and come to admire it." Confidence, faith (in what? just faith), a sense of passing with the perfection that passes (and does not pass), tireless, equal with itself. An instant is born, rises, opens out, vanishes at the moment when another instant is born and rises. Joy after joy. Ineffable abandonment and security. The vision of the gods is followed by nonvision: we're at the center of time. This trip is a return: a falling away, an unlearning, return to birth. Reading these pages of Michaux I remembered something the painter Paalen showed me some years ago: a chunk of quartz on which the image of old Tlaloc, the rain god, was incised. He went to the window and let the sun shine through it:

> Touched by the light
> The quartz becomes a cascade.
> On the waters floats the god, a child.

The nonvision: outside reality, history, purposes, calculations, hatred, love, "beyond resolutions and irresolutions, *beyond choices*," the poet returns to a perpetual birth and hears "the endless poem, without rhymes, without music, without words, which the Universe ceaselessly proclaims." The divine experience is participation in an infinite which is measure and rhythm. Inevitably the words water, music, light, great open space, resonant, come to the lips. The I vanishes but in the hollow it has left no other I takes its place. No god but rather the divine. No particular faith but rather the feeling that precedes and sustains all faith, all hope. No face but the being without face, the being which is all faces. Peace in the crater, reconciliation of man—what remains of him—with the total presence.

As he sets out on his experience, Michaux writes: "I intend to explore the mediocre human condition." That phrase—which can be applied as well to all of Michaux's work and to the work of any great artist—proved quite false in its second part. The exploration showed that man is not a mediocre creature. One part of him—walled up, obscured from the beginning of the beginning—is open to the infinite. The so-called human condition is a point at which other forces intersect. Perhaps our condition is not human.

Paris, 1961

II THE PRINCE AND THE CLOWN

To see is an act that postulates the ultimate identity between the beholder and the beheld. A postulate which needs neither proof nor demonstration: the eyes, when they see this or that, confirm the reality of what they see quite as much as their own reality. Mutual recognition: I recognize myself in what I recognize. To see is the original, paradisiac tautology. Mirror happiness: I discover myself in my images. What I look at is what looks: myself. A coincidence which unfolds: I am an image among my images and each of them, showing that it is real, confirms that I am real as well. . . . Soon, very soon, the coincidence breaks: I do not recognize myself in what I see nor do I recognize it. The world has taken leave of itself, gone I don't know where. There is no world. Or have I taken leave of myself? There is nowhere to go. There is a fault—in the geological sense: not a flaw but a fissure— and through it the images drain away. The eye recoils. One must extend a bridge, many bridges, between one shore of reality and the other, between beholder and beheld: language, languages. By those bridges we cross the null zones that divide this from that, here from there, now from before or after. But there are some who are obdurate—a few each century—who prefer not to move. They say that bridges do not exist or that movement is illusory; though we are ceaselessly restless and go from one place to another, in fact we have not changed places at all. Henri Michaux is one of those few. Fascinated, he approaches the edge of the precipice and, for many years now, gazes fixedly. What does he look at? The hollow, the wound, absence.

Whoever gazes at the fault is not seeking recognition. He does not look to confirm his reality in the reality of the world. Looking becomes a negation, an asceticism, a critical act. Looking as Michaux looks is to untie the knot of reflections into which the sense of sight has turned the world. To look in this fashion is to stanch the spring, the fountain of certainties at once radiant and meaningless, to break the mirror in which images, in self-contemplation, sip at themselves. To look with that gaze is to walk backward, unwalk the way one has come, go back until arrival at the end of all roads. To arrive at blackness. What is blackness? Michaux has written: "le noir ramene au fondement, a l'origine" ("black brings one back to the foundation, the origin"). But the origin is what draws further off as we approach it. It is a point on the line that describes a circle, and at that point, according to Heraclitus, beginning and periphery are confused together. Blackness is a foundation but also a precipice. Blackness is a well and the well is an eye. To gaze is not to recover the images that have fallen into the well of origin but to fall oneself into that well that is bottomless, without beginning. To fall into oneself, into one's eye, one's well. To contemplate in the pond, now waterless, the gradual evaporation of our shadow. Gazing thus is to witness the conjugations of blackness and the dispersions of transparency.

For Michaux painting has been a journey into himself, a spiritual descent. One trial, one passion. Also a lucid account of vertigo: during the interminable falling he kept his eyes open and was able to decipher, in the green and black stains on the sides of the well shaft, the inscriptions of fear, terror, madness. On a piece of paper, on his work table, by the light of a lamp, he saw a face, many faces: the solitude of the creature in threatening spaces. Journeys through the tunnels of the spirit and those of physiology, expeditions through the infinitesimal immensities of sensations, impressions, perceptions, representations. Histories, geographies, cosmologies of the countries of the interior, undefined, fluid, perpetually decomposing and gestating, with their ferocious vegetation, their spectral populations. Michaux is the painter of apparitions and disappearances. It is common, in considering his works, to praise his fantasy. I must confess that I am moved by their *accuracy*. They are true snapshots of horror, anxiety, dereliction. Or rather: we live among indefinable powers, but, though we do not know their true names, we know they take shape in sudden, momentary images, that they are horror, anguish, and despair *in person*. Michaux's creatures are unexpected revelations which, nonetheless, we recognize: we had already seen, in a gap of time, closing our eyes or turning our head, at an undefended moment, those atrocious and malevolent or suffering, vulnerable, and wounded features. Michaux does not invent: he sees. He astonishes us because he shows us what is hidden in the creases of our souls. All those creatures inhabit us, live and sleep with us. We are at the same time the fields they cultivate and their battlefields.

Michaux's painting shakes us because of its veracity: it is a witness that reveals the unreality of all realisms. What I have called, for lack of a better word, his *accuracy*, is a quality that appears in all the great visionaries. More than an aesthetic attribute it is a moral condition: it takes courage, integrity, purity, to look our monsters in the face. I spoke earlier of his lucidity; I should mention now its complement: forlornness. Alone, unarmed, defenseless, Michaux conjures the fearful powers. That is why his art—if that word can properly describe his poetic and graphic works—is also a proof. The artist, it has often been said, is a maker; in Michaux's case, that *making* is not only aesthetic. His pictures are not so much windows which let us view another reality as holes and openings perforated through by the powers on the other side. Space, in Michaux, is psychic. The picture is an exorcism more than a representation of the artist's visions. Michaux's familiarity with what we cannot but call the divine and demonic should not deceive us about the meaning of his enterprise. If he looks for an absolute, a beyond, that absolute does not bear the name of God; if he seeks a presence, that presence has neither face nor substance. His painting, like his poetry, is a struggle against phantoms, gods, and devils.

The bodily element has been no less decisive than the spiritual element in his graphic work. His exploration of "inner space" has coincided with his exploration of the materials and tools of the craft of painting. When he decided to try to express himself in graphic form, around 1937, he had not gone through the years of apprenticeship which are the obligatory course for painters. He had never spent time in an academy of art or taken drawing lessons. Hence the enraged character of many of his works. His relation with paper, canvas, colors, inks, molds, acids, pen and pencil, has not been that of the master with his tools, but that of one who grapples hand to hand with the unknown. These battles were a liberation. Michaux felt himself more secure, less oppressed by antecedents and precedents, by rules and by taste. What is surprising is that in his work there are no traces, even at the outset, of the awkwardnesses of the beginner. Was he in control of his means from the outset? On the contrary: from the outset he let himself be guided by them. His masters were the materials themselves. Nor is his painting barbarous, it is refined, with a refinement that does not exclude ferocity and humor. Fast, nervous painting, shaken by electric currents, painting with wings and beaks and claws. Michaux paints with the body, with all his senses together, mixed up, tensed, as if he wished to make the canvas the field of battle or of play for sensations and perceptions. Battle, play: also music. There is a rhythmic element in his painting. The hand sees, the eye hears. What does it hear? The surf of colors and inks, the whisper of lines which run together, the dry cries of the signs, insects that do battle on the leaves. The eye hears the circulation of the great impalpable forms in the empty spaces. Whirlwinds, whirlpools, explosions, migrations, floods, landslides, jungles, confabulations. Painting of movement, painting in movement.

The experience of drugs was also, in its way, a physical experience like the battle with his graphic materials. The result was, similarly, a psychic liberation. The well became a fountain. Mescaline released the flow of drawings, engravings, reflections, and notes in prose, poems. I have already spoken of Michaux's experiences of hallucinogenic drugs. As powerful as the action of the drugs—and more constant, since it has stayed with him through all of his adventures—has been the influence of humor. In current language the word *humor* has an almost entirely psychological meaning: a disposition of temperament and spirit. But humor is also a liquid, a substance, and thus it can be compared with drugs. In medieval and Renaissance medicine, the melancholy temperament depended not only on a disposition of spirit but on the combined influence of Saturn and black bile. The affinity between the melancholy temperament, a black "humor," and a predisposition to arts and letters fascinated the ancients. In the *Problems*, Aristotle affirms that in certain individuals "the seat of bile is near the seat of the intelligence and that is why fury and enthusiasm overcome them, as happens with Sybils and Bacchantes and with all those inspired by the gods. . . . Melancholics surpass other men in letters, the arts and public life." Among the great melancholics Aristotle cites are, preeminently, Heraclitus and Democritus. Ficino picks up this idea and weaves it together with the astrological motif of Saturn: "Melancholy or black bile fills the head with vapors, fires the brain and oppresses the spirit night and day with gloomy and frightening visions. . . ." From Ficino to Agrippa and from Agrippa to Dürer and his *Melencholia I*, Shakespeare and *Hamlet*, Donne, Juana Inés de la Cruz, the romantics, the symbolists . . . in the West melancholy has been the disease of the contemplative and spiritual.

In the composition—chemical and spiritual—of Michaux's black ink there is a Saturnine element. One of his earliest works is called *Prince of Night* (1937). It is a sumptuous and funereal character who, inevitably, calls to mind Nerval's Prince of Aquitaine of the sonnet "El desdichado." From almost the same period there is another gouache, its double and replica: *Clown*. The relation between Prince and Clown is intimate and ambiguous. It is the relationship between the hand and the cheek: "Je le gifle, je le gifle, je le mouche ensuite par dérision." That is also the relation between the sovereign and the subject: "Dans ma nuit, j'assiège mon Roi, je me lève progressivement et je lui tords le cou. Je le secoue et le secoue comme un vieux prunier, et sa couronne tremble sur sa tête. Et pourtant, c'est mon Roi. Je les sais et il le sait, et c'est bien sûr que je suis à son service." But who is the king and who is the clown? The secret of the identity of each character and of their transformations is in the black ink's well. The apparitions spring from the black and return to it. In the Western pictorial tradition humor does not abound, and the modern works in which it appears can be counted on the fingers, from Duchamp and Picabia to Klee and from Max Ernst to Matta. Michaux's intervention in this domain has been decisive and brilliant. The phosphorescent beings that spring from his well of black ink are no less surprising than those which rise out of the amphoras where djins are bottled up.

Michaux's earliest attempts at graphics were line drawings and "alphabets." The *sign* attracted him from the outset. A sign freed of its conceptual burden and closer, in the oral domain, to onomatopoeia than to the word. Painting and writing are cross-bred in Michaux without ever becoming confused. His poetry aspires to be pure rhythm, while his painting is shot through with the desire to say. In the first, a nostalgia for the line, in the second, for the word. But his poems, at the frontiers of Pentecost and silence, say; and his pictures, at the frontiers of saying, are silent. What his painting says cannot be translated to the language of poetry, and vice versa. All the same, both flow together: the same maelstrom fascinates them. World of apparitions, accumulations and dissolvings of forms, world of lines and arrows that riddle receding horizons: movement is continual metamorphosis, space unfolds, is dispersed, is scattered in animated fragments, joins back with itself, spins, is an incandescent ball which rolls across a blasted plain, stops at the edge of the paper, is a drop of ink pregnant with reptiles, is a drop of time that bursts and falls in a hard rain of seeds that lasts a thousand years. Michaux's creatures undergo all changes, from petrification to evaporation. Smoke hardens into mountain, stone is malleable and, if you blow on it, it vanishes, becomes a gust of air. Genesis, but genesis in reverse: forms, sucked at by the maelstrom, return to their origin. Forms falling toward their antique forms, embryonic, before the I and before language itself. Stains, jungles. Then, everything vanishes. Now we face the unlimited, what Michaux calls the "transreal." Before forms and names. The beyond of the visible which is also the beyond of the sayable. End of painting and of poetry. In a final metamorphosis Michaux's painting opens out and shows that, in truth, there is nothing to see. In that instant everything begins again: the unlimited is not outside but within us.

Mexico D.F., 6 October 1977

DOSTOEVSKI: THE DEVIL AND THE IDEOLOGUE

A century ago, on 28 January 1881, Feodor Dostoevski died. From that time his influence has grown and spread, first in his own country, where during his lifetime he had already achieved fame, and afterward in Europe, America, and Asia. This influence has not been exclusively literary but also spiritual and vital: several generations have read his novels not as fictions but as studies of the human soul, and hundreds of thousands of readers throughout the world have in imagination talked and argued with his characters as if they were old acquaintances. His work has touched spirits as different as Nietzsche and Gide, Faulkner and Camus; in Mexico two writers read him with passion, no doubt because they belonged to his own intellectual family and recognized themselves in many of his ideas and obsessions: Vasconcelos and Revueltas. He is (or was) a writer preferred by the young: I still remember the endless conversations I carried on, when I was finishing my B.A., with some of my classmates on long walks which began at nightfall in San Ildefonso and ended after midnight in Santa Maria or on Avenida de los Insurgentes, looking out for the last tram. Ivan and Dimitri Karamazov fought it out in each one of us.

Nothing was more natural than that fervor: despite the century which divides us from him, Dostoevski is our great contemporary. Very few writers of the past have his presence: to read his novels is to read a chronicle of the twentieth century. But his presence is not that of intellectual or literary novelty. In his tastes and his aesthetic concerns he is a writer of another age; he is prolix, and, were it not for his oddly modern humor, many of his pages would be boring. His historical world is not ours. *Diary of a Writer* contains many passages which repel me with their Slavism and their anti-Semitism. His anti-European tirades remind me, though they are more inspired than these, of the ventings and resentments of Mexican and Latin American nationalism. His vision of history is sometimes profound but also confused: it lacks that understanding of event, at once quick and sharp, which delights us in a writer like Stendhal. Nor did he have the eye of Tocqueville, which sees through the surface of a society and an age. He was not, like Tolstoi, an epic chronicler. He does not tell us what happens but he obliges us to go down under ground so that we see *what is* happening really: he obliges us to see ourselves. Dostoevski is our contemporary because he guessed what the dramas and conflicts of our age would be. And he guessed not because he had the gift of prophecy or was able to see future events, but because he had the ability to get inside souls.

He was one of the first—perhaps *the* first—who took account of modern nihilism. He has left us descriptions of that spiritual phenomenon which are unforgettable and which, even today, shake us with their insight and their mysterious precision. The nihilism of antiquity was related to skepticism and epicureanism;

his ideal was a noble serenity: to achieve equanimity despite the accidents of fortune. The nihilism of ancient India, which so impressed Alexander and his companions, according to Plutarch, was a philosophical attitude not without analogy to pyrrhonism and which culminated in the contemplation of vacuity. For Nāgārjuna and his followers, nihilism was the antechamber of religion.

But modern nihilism, though it too is born of intellectual conviction, does not open out into philosophical impassivity or the beatitude of indifference; rather, it is an inability to believe or affirm something, a spiritual more than a philosophical failure. Nietzsche imagined the coming of a "complete nihilist," embodied in the Superman, who plays, dances, and laughs in the spirals of the Eternal Return. The Superman's dance celebrates universal *insignificance*, the evaporation of meaning and the subversion of values. But the true nihilist, as Dostoevski saw more realistically, neither dances nor laughs: he goes from here to there—around his room or, it's the same to him, around the world—without ever being able to rest but also without being able to do anything. He is condemned to go round and round, talking to his phantoms. His sickness, like that of Sade's libertines or the *accidie* of the medieval monks, attacked by the midday devil, is a continual dissatisfaction, an inability to love anyone or anything, a restlessness without object, a disgust of the self— and a love of the self. The modern nihilist, poor Narcissus, sees in the water's depth his reflection shattered into pieces. The vision of his fall fascinates him: faced with himself, nausea grips him, but he cannot look away. Quevedo guessed at this state in two lines that are hard to forget: "las aguas del abismo / donde me enamoraba de mi mismo" ("the waters of the abyss where I was falling in love with myself").

Stavrogin, protagonist of *The Devils* (less literal—the old translation *The Possessed* was more exact), writes to Daria Pavlovna, who loved him: "I have set trials, everywhere, for my strength. . . . During these trials, before myself or before the others, that strength has always proven limitless. But, what to do with it? This is what I never knew and still don't know, despite all the courage you want to give me. . . . I can feel the desire to carry through a good deed and this pleases me; and yet I feel the same pleasure when I want to do something bad . . . my feelings are petty, never strong. . . . I threw myself into the life of a libertine . . . but I do not love or even like licentiousness. . . . Do you believe because you love me, that you could give some purpose to my existence? Do not be imprudent: my love is as feeble as I am. . . . Your brother told me one day that whoever has no more ties with the earth loses his gods forthwith. That's to say, his purposes. One can argue all of this indefinitely but I can only deny, deny without the least grandeur of soul, without strength. In me, denial itself is feeble. All is spongy, bland. Generous Kirilov couldn't bear *his idea* and he blew off the top of his head. . . . I could never lose my mind or believe in an idea, the way he did. . . . I could never, never, shoot myself in the temple." How to define this situation? Dispiritedness, lack of spirit. Stavrogin: the man whose soul has been removed.

Yet having written that letter, Stavrogin hangs himself in the garret. The final paradox: the noose was made of silk and the suicide, with foresight, carefully, had soaped it. Fascination with death and fear of pain. But the greatness of the nihilist resides not in his attitude nor in his ideas but in his lucidity. His clarity redeems him from what Stavrogin called his baseness or pettiness. Or is suicide, far from being an answer, another test? If that is so, it is an inadequate test. No matter: the nihilist is an intellectual hero, since he dares to delve into his cloven soul, in the knowledge that he's engaged in a hopeless exploration. Nietzsche would say that Stavrogin was an "incomplete nihilist": he lacks knowledge of the Eternal Return. But perhaps it would be more precise to say that Dostoevski's character, like so many of our contemporaries, is an incomplete Christian. He has ceased believing but he has been unable to substitute others for the ancient certitudes or to live in the open, without ideas to justify or give meaning to his existence. God has disappeared, but evil has not. The loss of metaphysical referents does not extinguish sin: on the contrary, it gives it a kind of immortality. The nihilist is nearer to Gnostic pessimism than to Christian optimism and the hope of salvation. If there is no God there is no remission of sins, but evil is not abolished either: sin ceases to be an accident, a state, and becomes a permanent condition of men. It is a reversal of Augustinianism: evil is being. The utopian would like to bring heaven to earth, and make us gods; the nihilist knows himself condemned from birth; earth is already hell.

The portrait of the nihilist, is it a self-portrait? Yes and no: Dostoevski writes to escape nihilism not by suicide and negation but by affirmation and joy. The answer to nihilism, that disease of intellectuals, is the vital simplicity of Dimitri Karamazov or the supernatural joy of Alyosha. One way or the other, the answer is not in philosophy and ideas but in life. The refutation of nihilism in the innocence of the simple. Dostoevski's world is peopled by men, women, and children who are at once commonplace and prodigious. Some are anguished, others sensual, some sing in their abjection and others despair in their prosperity. There are saints and criminals, idiots and geniuses, women pious as a glass of water, and children who are angels tormented by their parents. (How different Dostoevski's vision of childhood is from Freud's!) A world of criminals and just men: for both the gates of the kingdom of heaven are open. All can save or lose themselves. The corpse of Father Zosima exhales a stench of corruption, revealing that, despite his piety, he did not die in the odor of sanctity; on the other hand, remembering the bandits and criminals who were his companions in prison in Siberia, Dostoevski says: "There man, quite soon, escapes all measure." Man, "improbable creature," can save himself at any moment. In this, Dostoevski's Christianity is kin to the ideas on liberty and grace of Calderón, Tirso de Molina, and Mira de Amescua.

For us, Dostoevski's saints and prostitutes, criminals and just men possess an almost superhuman reality; I mean to say, they are unusual beings, from another age. An age on its way to extinction: they belong to the preindustrial era. In this sense Marx was the more lucid: he foresaw the disintegration of the traditional bonds and the erosion of old ways of life by the combined action of the capitalist market and industry. But Marx did not predict the rise of a new type of men who, though calling themselves his heirs, would bring about in the twentieth century the ruin of socialist dreams and aspirations. Dostoevski was the first to describe this class of men. We know them well since in our day their number is legion: they are the sectarians and fanatics of ideology, proselytes of the Stavrogins and Ivans of our time. Their prototype is Smerdiakov, the parricide, disciple of Ivan and precursor of Stalin and so many others. The sectarians have inherited from the nihilists not their lucidity but their lack of belief. And they have converted lack of belief into a new and more base superstition. Dostoevski calls them the *possessed* because, unlike Ivan and Stavrogin, they are not aware that they are possessed by devils. That is why he compares them to the pigs in the Gospel (Luke 7:31–35). When they lose their old faith, they venerate falsely rational idols: progress, social and revolutionary utopias. They have forsworn their parents' religion, but not religion itself: instead of Christ and the Virgin Mary they adore two or three ideas out of a pamphlet. They're the ancestors of our terrorists. Dostoevski's world is that of a society sick with that corruption of religion which we call ideology. His world is the prefiguration of ours.

Dostoevski was a revolutionary in his youth. He was imprisoned for his activities, sentenced to death, and then pardoned. He spent several years in Siberia—the concentration camps of modern Russia are a perfected and amplified inheritance of the czarist system of repression—and on his return he broke with his radical past. He was conservative, Christian, monarchist, and nationalist. Even so, it would be wrong to reduce his work to an ideological definition. He was not an ideologue—though ideas have a cardinal importance in his novels—but a novelist. One of his protagonists, Dimitri Karamazov, says: *We should love life more than the sense of life.* Dimitri is an answer to Ivan, but not *the* answer: Dostoevski does not oppose one idea to another, but one human reality to another. As was not the case with Flaubert, James, or Proust, ideas are real for him, though not in themselves but as a dimension of existence. The only ideas that interested him were embodied ideas. Some come from God, that is to say, from the depth of the heart; others, the majority, come from the devil, that is to say, from the brain. As the soul was for medieval clergymen, conscience for the modern intellectual is a theater of war. The novels of Dostoevski, from this perspective, are religious parables, and his art is closer to Saint Augustine and Pascal than to modern realism. At the same time, on account of the rigor of his psychological analyses, his work anticipates Freud and, in certain ways, transcends him.

We owe to Dostoevski the most profound and comprehensive diagnosis of the modern disease: psychic schism, the divided conscience. His description is psychological and religious at the same time. Stavrogin and Ivan suffer visions: they see and speak to specters which are devils. At the same time, since both are modern, they attribute those apparitions to psychic blockages: they are projections of their troubled souls. But neither of them is very sure of that explanation. Time and again, in their conversation with their spectral visitants, they find themselves constrained to accept their reality in desperation: they really converse with the devil. The consciousness of the schism is diabolical: to be possessed means to know that the "I" is broken and there is a stranger who usurps our voice. Is that stranger the devil or ourselves? Whatever we reply, the identity of the person is divided. These passages are like hallucinations: Ivan's and Stavrogin's conversations with their devils are recounted with great realism and as if the subject were commonplace. Absurd situations and ironic reflections abound. By turns fear makes us laugh, then makes our blood run cold. We experience an ambiguous fascination: the psychological description turns imperceptibly into metaphysical speculation, this into religious vision, and, at last, religious vision into a story that mingles in an inexplicable way the supernatural and the everyday, the grotesque and the abysmal.

Dostoevski's devils are uniquely credible in modern literature. Since the eighteenth century the phantoms of our poems and novels have been unconvincing. They are comic figures, and the affectation of their language and attitudes is, at the same time, pompous and intolerable. The devils of Goethe and Valéry are plausible because of their extremely intellectual and symbolic character; acceptable too are those which present themselves in a deliberate and ironic manner as fantastic fictions: the devil in Nerval's *The Enchanted Hand* or the delicious *Devil in Love* of Cazotte. But modern devils brag of being devils and do all they can to let us know they come from there, from the underworld. They are the parvenus of the supernatural. Dostoevski's devils are modern, too, and don't resemble the old medieval and baroque devils, lascivious, extravagant, astute, and a little stupid. Dostoevski's devils are our contemporaries and possess a *clinical* reality, to put it that way. This is his great discovery: he saw the hidden resemblance between evil and infirmity, possession and reflection. His devils reason, and, as if they were psychoanalysts, they endeavor to prove their nonexistence, their imaginary nature. They tell us: I'm nothing but an obsession. And then: I am the nothing that manifests itself as obsession. I am your obsession; I am your nothing. They triumph over us (and themselves) thanks to these unanswerable arguments. Ivan and Stavrogin, two intellectuals, have no choice but to believe them: they are truly the devil since only the devil can reason in that way. But they would also be possessed by the devil if they clung to the belief that it's merely a matter of a sick mind's hallucinations. In either case, both are possessed by denial, the devil's essence. This is how the thought that terrorizes Ivan is fulfilled: to believe in the devil it is not necessary to believe in God.

There is one kind of person immune to the seduction of the devil: the ideologue. He is the man who has rooted out duality. He does not discuss: he demonstrates, indoctrinates, refutes, convinces, condemns. He calls others *comrades* but he never talks to them: he talks to *his idea*. Nor does he speak to the *other* which we all carry within us. He doesn't even suspect its existence: the *other* is an idealist fantasy, a petit-bourgeois superstition. The ideologue is the spiritual cripple: half of him is missing. Dostoevski loved the poor and the simple, the humbled and those who had been sinned against, but he never concealed his antipathy for those who called themselves their saviors. Their "pretense to want to free man from the burden of liberty" struck him as absurd. A terrible and valuable burden. The ideologists have responded to his dislike with their own, no less intense. In a letter to his friend Ines Armand, Lenin calls him "the arch-mediocre Dostoevski." On another occasion he said: "I don't waste time on trash." In the Stalin era he was almost a forbidden author, and even today, in official circles, he is seen as a reactionary and an enemy. Despite government hostility, his books are the most widely read in Russia, especially among students, intellectuals, and, of course, detainees in concentration camps.

The tyrant is arbitrary and capricious; against the excesses of mad and unbalanced men like Nero and Caligula, the traditional remedy has been the regicide's dagger. It is useless against ideological despotism, which is systematic and impersonal: one cannot assassinate an abstraction. But ideology, which is immune to bullets, is not immune to criticism. Thus the ideological despot knows only two forms of expression: monologue and lecture. The tyranny of the ideologue is the soliloquy of a sadistic and pedantic professor, intent on making society a square and each man a triangle. For this reason, quite apart from the permanent fascination we feel for his work, Dostoevski is real. His reality is moral and political: he teaches us that society is not a blackboard and that man, unpredictable creature that he is, eludes all definitions, compulsions, even those of the tyrant turned geometrician.

Mexico, 1981

Considering
Solzhenitsyn:
Dust After Mud

*I have often heard it said that cowardice is the
mother of cruelty.*

—Montaigne

In 1947 I was reading, with a chill in my soul, David Rousset's
book on Hitler's concentration camps, *The Days of Our Death*.
Rousset's book impressed me for two reasons: it was the account
of a victim of the Nazis, but at the same time a lucid social and
psychological analysis of that separate universe, the twentieth-
century concentration camps. Two years later Rousset published
in the French press another declaration: the industry of homicide
was flourishing in the Soviet Union as well. Many received Rousset's revelations with the horror and disbelief of one who suddenly
discovers a hidden leprosy in Venus Aphrodite. The Communists
and their comrades responded angrily: Rousset's allegations were
a crude invention of the CIA and the propaganda services of
American imperialism. "Progressive" intellectuals behaved no better
than the Communists. In the magazine *Les temps modernes* Jean-

Paul Sartre and Maurice Merleau-Ponty adopted a curious attitude (see issues 51 and 57 of that magazine, January and July
1950). Neither philosopher attempted to deny the deeds nor to
minimize their seriousness, but both refused to draw the conclu-
sions which the existence of the camps compelled on reflection:
to what degree was Stalinist totalitarianism the result—as much
as or more than of Russia's social backwardness and autocratic
past—of the Leninist concept of the Party? Were not Stalin and
his forced-labor camps the product of the terrorist, antidemo-
cratic practices of the Bolsheviks from the time they took power
in 1917?

Years later, Merleau-Ponty attempted to answer those questions in *The Adventures of Dialectics*, a partial corrective for a
book which, at the end of his life, he very much regretted having
written: *Humanism and Terror*. And Sartre: we know his views.
Even in 1974 he asserts, though he deplores it, the inevitability
both of violence and of dictatorship. Not of a class but of a
group:

> . . . violence is necessary to change from one society to another
> but I do not know the nature of the order which, perhaps, will
> replace the present society. Will there be a dictatorship of the
> proletariat? To tell the truth, I don't believe so. There will
> always be a dictatorship exercised by representatives of the
> proletariat, which is something entirely different. . . . (*Le monde*,
> 8 February 1974)

Sartre's pessimism has one advantage at least: it puts the cards
on the table. But in 1950, trapped in a dilemma we now know
was false, both French writers decided to condemn David Rousset: in denouncing the repressive Soviet system in the major bourgeois newspapers, their old companion had become a tool of the
cold war and provided weapons for the enemies of socialism.

In those years I lived in Paris. The polemics on the Russian concentration camps moved and shook me: they put under interdict the validity of an historical enterprise that had kindled the minds of the best men of our time. The 1917 Revolution, as André Breton wrote some time before, was a fabulous beast similar to the zodiacal Aries: "Though violence nested between its horns, the whole of springtime opened in the depths of its eyes." Now those eyes observed us with the vacant gaze of the murderer. I made a summary and a selection of documents and testimonies which proved, without grounds for doubt, the existence in the USSR of a vast repressive system, founded on the forced labor of millions of human beings and integrated into the Soviet economy. Victoria Ocampo, the distinguished editor of the Argentinean magazine *Sur*, learned of my work and revealed her ethical consistency and integrity once again: she asked me to send the documentary evidence I had collected for publication in *Sur*, along with a brief explanatory note (see *Sur*, number 19, March 1951). The reaction of progressive intellectuals was silence. No one mentioned my article, but a campaign of insinuation recurred, along with misleading suggestions initiated some years earlier by Neruda and his Mexican friends. It was a campaign that dogs me even today. The epithets change, but not the reproach: I have been successively a "cosmopolitan," "formalist," "Trotskyite," CIA agent, "liberal intellectual," and even a "structuralist at the service of the bourgeoisie"!

My commentary on the facts advanced the usual explanation: the Soviet concentration camps were a blemish that disfigured the Russian regime but did not amount to an inherent flaw in the system. To say that, in 1950, was a political error; to repeat it now, in 1974, would be something more than an error. What most impressed me, and the majority of those who in those years took an interest in the matter, was the economic function of the forced-labor camps. I believed that, unlike the Nazi camps—real extermination camps—the Soviet camps were a wicked form of exploitation, not without analogies to Stakhanovism. One of the "spurs of industrialization." I was wrong: now we know that the mortality rate in the camps, shortly before the Second World War, was 40 percent of the interned population, while the productivity of a camp laborer was 50 percent that of a free laborer (see Hannah Arendt, *Le système totalitaire*, p. 281, Paris, 1972). The publication of Robert Conquest's work on the great purges (*The Great Terror*, London, 1968) completes the accounts and testimonies of the survivors—the majority of them Communists—and closes the debate. Or, better said, opens it on another plane. The function of the camps was *something else*.

If the economic usefulness of the camps is more than doubtful, their political function presents peculiarities at once strange and repugnant. The camps are not a weapon in the battle against political enemies but an institution of punishment for the vanquished. The person who ends up in a camp is not an active opponent but a defeated man, defenseless and unable to offer further resistance. The same logic rules the purges and purifications: they aren't incidents in political and ideological battles but immense ceremonies of expiation and punishment. The confessions and self-accusations turn the defeated into the accomplices of their executioners, and thus the grave itself becomes a rubbish collector. Saddest of all, the majority of the internees were not (and are not) political opponents: they are "delinquents" from every level of Soviet society. In Stalin's time the population of the camps came to exceed fifteen million human beings. It has diminished since the liberal reforms of Khrushchev and today it varies between one and two million persons, of whom—according to the experts on these melancholy matters—only some ten thousand can be considered political prisoners, in the strict sense of the word. It is incredible that the rest—a million human beings—should be made up of delinquents, at any event in the sense we in our countries give to that term. The political and psychological function of the camps becomes clear: it is a matter of an institution of *preventive terror*, for lack of a better expression. The entire populace, even under the relatively more humane rule of Khrushchev and his successors, lives under threat of internment. A staggering transposition of the dogma of original sin: each Soviet citizen can be transported to a forced-labor camp. The communization of guilt includes the communization of punishment.

THE PUBLICATION of *The Gulag Archipelago*, and the campaign of defamation against Alexander Solzhenitsyn which culminated in his expulsion from the Soviet Union, tested again, as in 1950, the disposition and the independence of writers throughout the world. Among us in Latin America, a few protested, others kept silence; others disgraced themselves. A modish fellow who nowadays, on the official Mexican television network, sucks up to the bureaucracy that rules us and at the same time to the intellectuals that criticize it, didn't hesitate to pillory Solzhenitsyn: in the name of "abstract liberty" the Russian dissident had defamed the "most important social experiment of the twentieth century." According to this two-face, the Russian dissidents want to return to a free-enterprise system, while the defenders of real liberty are Brezhnev and Father Arrupe, Captain General of the Jesuits, who is a declared enemy of the capitalist system! The majority of Mexican writers and journalists who have concerned themselves with Solzhenitsyn have done so with more discretion, dignity, and generosity. Nonetheless, few have spoken as frankly and courageously as José Revueltas. The Mexican novelist has revealed, once again, that revolutionary convictions are not at loggerheads with a love of truth and that a scrutiny of what occurs in countries called "socialist" itself requires a revision of the authoritarian legacy of Marxism. A revision which, I add in passing, ought to go beyond Lenin and probe the Hegelian origins of Marx's thought.

The writer of *Inventario*, the acute and almost always judicious chronicle of *Diorama de la cultura*, probably with the intention of defending Solzhenitsyn against the snapping of the rabid pack, recalled that Lukács had, at the end of his life, considered Solzhenitsyn a true "socialist realist." I quote that paragraph:

> Lukács presents the author of *The First Circle* as the most achieved exponent of socialist realism who has, socially and ideologically, the chance of discovering all the immediate and concrete aspects of society, and representing them artistically according to the laws of their own evaluation.

In the speech he wrote accepting the 1970 Nobel Prize, Solzhenitsyn spoke a few words which can summarize what Lukács meant by socialist realism, something quite distinct from those propaganda texts disguised as novels which are not realistic and much less socialist:

> Literature is the memory of peoples; it transmits from one generation to the next the irrefutable experiences of men. It preserves and enlivens the flame of a history immune to all deformation, far from every lie.

Before this strange opinion, two comments occur to me. First: since its origins in 1934 "socialist realism" has been a literary-bureaucratic dogma of Stalinism, while Solzhenitsyn, a rebel writer, is more an heir to the realism of Tolstoi and Dostoevski, profoundly Slavic and Christian. Second: even if Solzhenitsyn were a "socialist realist" who does not know he is a "socialist realist," *The Gulag Archipelago* is not a novel but a work of history.

The Gulag Archipelago is not only a denunciation of the excesses of the Stalinist regime, however atrocious they may have been, but of the Soviet system itself, as it was established by Lenin and the Bolsheviks. There are two dates that form an essential part of the title of the book and its content: *1918–1956*. The work extends from the origins of the Soviet system of repression (the establishment of the Cheka in 1918) to the beginning of Khrushchev's regime. We know, moreover, that in other volumes not yet published the Russian writer concerns himself with repression in the contemporary period, that is, the period of Khrushchev and Brezhnev. Solzhenitsyn's opinions are, of course, open to dispute. See for example Roy Medvedev's criticism from the perspective of Marxism-Leninism. The Russian historian agrees that it would not be honest to conceal the serious errors of Lenin but thinks that those errors do not compromise entirely the Bolshevik historical project. Medvedev's position isn't very far from that which Merleau-Ponty and Sartre assumed in 1950, though he does not concur in the bigotry of the pious legend of the Bolsheviks. ("In Lenin and Trotsky," declared the editorial in *Les temps modernes* 51, "there isn't a single word that isn't sensible.") Halfway between Solzhenitsyn and Medvedev we find Sakharov, the great physicist and mathematician. His condemnation of Leninism is more decisive than Medvedev's, but in his criticism there is neither Slavophilia nor Christianity as in Solzhenitsyn's work. Sakharov is a liberal intellectual, in the true sense of the expression, and is closer to Herzen and Turgenev than to Dostoevski and Tolstoi.

This brief description reveals the variety of the Soviet dissidents' attitudes. A really remarkable feat is the survival—or more correctly, the continued vitality—of intellectual and spiritual currents predating the 1917 Revolution, and these, after half a century of Marxist-Leninist dictatorship, reappear and inspire men as different as the historian Andrei Amalrik and the poet Joseph Brodsky. Amalrik's historical analyses owe little to the Marxist method, and Brodsky's thought is profoundly marked by the Judaic-Christian philosophy of Leon Chestov. In fact, we are present at the resurrection of the old Russian culture. I indicated above the liberal and Europeanist affiliation of Sakharov, in the tradition of Herzen. On the other hand, Solzhenitsyn's thought is part of the tradition of that philosophical Christian current which Vladimir Soloviev (1853–1900) represented toward the end of the last century. The position the Medvedev brothers adopt is, too, an indication that a certain "Western Marxism," a social-democratic Marxism, closer to the thought of the Mensheviks than the ideas of Lenin and Trotsky, did not perish in exile with Plekanov and Martov.

The first sign of the resurrection of Russian culture, at least for us foreigners, was the publication of Pasternak's *Dr. Zhivago*. The reader will perhaps recall that in the early chapters there are allusions to the ideas and even to the persons of Soloviev and Vyacheslav Ivanov. The figure of Lara, a fusion of Russia and woman, instantly calls to mind the erotic-religious-patriotic vision of Soloviev and the cult of Sophia. Pasternak's fascination is not unique. In his youth Soloviev had so impressed Dostoevski that some of his characteristics reappear in Alyosha Karamazov. Later on the philosopher was to leave his mark on Aleksandr Blok and today he influences Solzhenitsyn. But the Russian novelist aligns himself more closely with the tradition of exalted religiousness and Slavophilia of a Seraph of Sarov and of a Tikhon Zadonsky, rather as the Patriarch Zosima is its incarnation in Dostoevski's novel (cf. *The Icon and the Axe*, James H. Billington, New York, 1968). In Solzhenitsyn there is no Russian imperialism; but there is a clear repugnance for the West, its rationalism, and its materialist democracy of soulless businessmen. On the other hand, Soloviev never concealed his sympathies with Roman Catholicism and European civilization. His two masters are, however strange it may seem, Joseph de Maistre and Auguste Comte. The actuality of Soloviev is extraordinary. Doubtless readers of *Plural* will recall the essay by the great Polish poet Czeslaw Milosz about one of his works: *Three Conversations on War, Progress, and the End of the World, with a Brief History of the Antichrist and Supplements* (*Plural*, 12 September 1972). In that celebrated work Soloviev prophesies, among other things, the

110

Sino-Soviet conflict, a conflict in which he saw, not without reason, the beginning of the end.

To explore relations between the spiritual history of Russia and the contemporary dissidents is a labor beyond the limits both of this essay and of my ability. Nor have I set out to describe the ideas of Solzhenitsyn, still less to defend or attack them. The temper of that writer, the depth of his feelings, and the uprightness and integrity of his character awake spontaneously my admiration, but that admiration does not imply an adherence to his philosophy. True, as well as a moral sympathy, I feel a certain affinity with him too, a spiritual rather than an intellectual affinity. Solzhenitsyn is not only a critic of Russia and Bolshevism but of the modern age itself. What does it matter if that critique proceeds from presuppositions different from mine? Another Soviet dissident, the poet Brodsky, said to me recently in Cambridge, Massachusetts, "It all began with Descartes." I could have shrugged my shoulders and replied, "It all began with Hume . . . or Kant." I preferred to remain silent and reflect on the atrocious history of the twentieth century. I don't know when it all began; I ask myself, when will it end? Solzhenitsyn's critique is neither more profound nor more true than Thoreau's, Blake's, or Nietzsche's. Nor does it invalidate what, in our days, the great poets and rebels have said. I think of those irreducible and incorruptible figures—Breton, Russell, Camus, and a few others, some now dead, others surviving, who did not yield and have not yielded to the totalitarian blandishments of communism or fascism or the "comfort" of the consumer society. Solzhenitsyn speaks from another tradition, and this, for me, is impressive: his voice is not modern but ancient. It is an ancientness tempered in the modern world. His ancientness is that of the old Russian Christianity, but it is a Christianity which has passed through the central experience of our century—the dehumanization of the totalitarian concentration camps—and has emerged intact and strengthened. If history is the testing ground, Solzhenitsyn has passed the test. His example is not intellectual or political nor even, in the current sense of the word, moral. We have to use an even older word, a word which still retains a religious overtone—a hint of death and sacrifice: *witness*. In a century of false testimonies, a writer becomes the witness to man.

Solzhenitsyn's ideas—religious, political, and literary—are disputable, but I will not dispute them here. His book raises issues which go beyond, on the one hand, his political philosophy and, on the other, the ritual condemnation of Stalinism. This latter issue concerns me. The Bolshevik program, that is, Marxism-Leninism, is a universal program, and from that derives the interest, for non-Russian readers, of Solzhenitsyn's book. *The Gulag Archipelago* isn't a book of political philosophy but a work of history; more precisely, it is a *witnessing*—in the old sense of the word: the martyrs are witnesses—to the repressive system founded in 1918 by the Bolsheviks and which survives intact down to our days, though it has been relatively humanized by Khrushchev and does not today display the monstrous and grotesque traces of Stalinism.

THE TERROR OF THE JACOBINS was a temporary, emergency measure, an extraordinary recourse to meet the challenge of internal insurrection and external aggression at the same time. The Bolshevik terror began in 1918 and endures today: over half a century. In *The State and Revolution*, a book written in 1917, shortly before the attack on the Winter Palace, Lenin opposed the ideas of Karl Kautsky and the theses of the Second International—those tendencies seemed to him authoritarian and bureaucratic—and delivered an exalted eulogy of political liberty and of self-government by the workers. *The State and Revolution* contradicts many of Lenin's earlier opinions and, more decisively and significantly, all his practice from the time that his Bolshevik Party took power. Between the Leninist concept of the Bolshevik

Party, "the vanguard of the proletariat," and the ardent semi-anarchism of *The State and Revolution* there is an abyss. The figure of Lenin, like all human figures, is contradictory and dramatic: the author of *The State and Revolution* was also the founder of the Cheka and the forced-labor camps, and the man who initiated the dictatorship of the Central Committee over the Party.

Would Lenin, had he survived longer, have accomplished the democratic reform of both the Party and the regime itself? We cannot know. In his so-called Will he suggested that, to avoid a bureaucratic dictatorship, the number of members of the Central Committee of the Politburo should be increased. Rather like applying a poultice to cure a cancer. The evil was not (and is not) only in the dictatorship by the Committee over the Party but of the Party over the country. In any case, Lenin's suggestion was not taken up: the Politburo of 1974 is composed, like that of 1918, of eleven members, over which a Secretary General reigns. Nor did the other Bolshevik leaders reveal an understanding of the political problem, and all of them confused in a common scorn what they called "bourgeois democracy" and human liberty. Thanks perhaps to the influence of Bukharin, Lenin adopted a political program called NEP, which saved Russia from the great economic crisis which followed the civil war. But neither Lenin nor Bukharin thought of applying the NEP's economic liberalism to political life. Let's listen to Bukharin: "Among us too other parties can exist. But here—and this is the fundamental principle that distinguishes us from the West—the only conceivable situation is this: one party rules, the others are in prison" (*Troud*, 13 November 1927). This statement is not exceptional. In 1921 Lenin said, "The place for the Mensheviks and Revolutionary Socialists, both those who admit to it and those who conceal it, is prison. . . ." And to clear up any confusion between the economic liberalism of the NEP and political liberalism, Lenin writes to Kamenev in a letter dated 3 November 1922: "It is a big mistake to believe that the NEP has put an end to terror. We will have recourse to terror again and also to economic terror."

The majority of historians believe that the road which led to the Stalinist perversion began with the change from the dictatorship of the Soviets (councils of workers, farmers, and soldiers) to the dictatorship of the Party. Nonetheless, some forget that the theoretical justification of that confusion between the organs of the working class and the Party constitutes the very marrow of Leninism. Without the Party, Lenin said, there is no proletarian revolution: "The history of all nations shows that, by its own efforts, the working class is not capable of evolving beyond a syndicalist conscience." Lenin turns the working class into a minor, and makes the Party the true agent of history. In 1904, Trotsky commanded these ideas and anticipated the whole process, from the phase where the Party is above the proletariat to the phase in which the Central Committee is above the Party, and afterward to the phase in which the Politburo is above the Committee, until we reach the phase in which a dictator is above the Politburo.

Later Trotsky succumbed to the same aberration he had denounced. With his habitual clarity and coherence, in *Terrorism and Communism* (1920), he applied the Leninist ideas of the function of the "vanguard" of the Party:

> We have been accused more than once of substituting the Party dictatorship for the dictatorship of the Soviets. Nonetheless, we can affirm without risk of error that the dictatorship of the Soviets has not been possible without the dictatorship of the Party.... The substitution of the power of the working class by the power of the Party has not been a fortuitous or chance occurrence: the Communists express the fundamental interests of the working class.... But, some cunning critics ask, who guarantees that it is precisely *your* Party that expresses the historical evolution? In suppressing or repressing the other parties, you have eliminated political rivalry, the source of positive contention, and thus you have deprived yourselves of the possibility of verifying the soundness of the political line you have

adopted. . . . This critique is inspired by a purely liberal idea of the course of the revolution. . . . We have crushed the Mensheviks and the Revolutionary Socialists, and that judgment is enough for us. In any case our task is not to measure each moment, statistically, the importance of the groups that represent each tendency, but to make certain of the victory of our tendency, which is the tendency of the dictatorship of the proletariat. . . .

To justify the dictatorship of the Party over the Soviets, Trotsky substitutes the quantitative and objective criterion—that is, the democratic criterion which consists in "measuring" what tendencies represent the majority and what the minority—with a qualitative, subjective criterion: the supposed ability of the Party to interpret the "true" interests of the masses, even if against the opinion and will of these.

In the last great political debate within the Bolshevik Party which ended with the destruction of the so-called Workers' Opposition (Tenth Party Congress, 1921), Trotsky said:

The Workers' Opposition has made fetishes of democratic principles. It has placed the right of the workers to elect their representatives above Party, to put it in those terms, as though the Party hadn't the right to impose its dictatorship, even if that dictatorship were temporarily to oppose the changing tendencies of workers' democracy. We must remember the historical revolutionary mission of the Party. The Party is obliged to maintain its dictatorship without bearing in mind the ephemeral fluctuations of spontaneous reactions among the masses and even the momentary vacillation of the working class. . . . The dictatorship does not rest at every moment on the formal principle of workers' democracy.

In his Will Lenin reproaches Trotsky for his arrogance ("he has too much confidence in himself") and his bureaucratic tendencies ("he is too much inclined not to consider any but the purely administrative side of things"). But Lenin did not remark that those tendencies of Trotsky's personality had been justified in and nourished by the same ideas as his own on the relationship between the Party and the working classes. The same can be said of the personal tendencies of Bukharin and Stalin: Leninism was their common theoretical and political foundation. I do not wish to compare two eminent but tragically and radically wrongheaded men, Bukharin and Trotsky, with a monster like Stalin. I only point out their common intellectual affiliation.

The Leninist notion of political power is inseparable from the notion of dictatorship; and this, in turn, is conducive to terror. Lenin was the creator of the Cheka, and the Bolsheviks of the historic period were the first to justify the execution of hostages, the mass deportations, and the liquidation of whole collectives. Before Stalin murdered the Bolsheviks, Lenin and Trotsky physically annihilated, by violent and lawless means, the other revolutionary parties, from the Mensheviks to the Anarchists and from the Revolutionary Socialists to the left-wing Communist opposition. Years later, in exile, Trotsky repented, though only in part, and conceded, in *The Betrayed Revolution* (1936), that the first thing that had to be done in Russia was to re-establish the legality of other revolutionary parties. Why only the *revolutionary* parties?

In Marxism there were authoritarian tendencies that had their origin in Hegel. Yet Marx never spoke of the dictatorship of a single party, but of something very different: temporary dictatorship of the proletariat in the period directly after the taking of power. Leninism introduced a new element: the notion of the revolutionary party, the vanguard of the proletariat, which implies in its name the course of society and history. The essence of Leninism is not in the generous ideas of *The State and Revolution*, which appears too in other socialist and anarchist authors, but in the concept of a party of professional revolutionaries which embodies the march of history. This party tends to turn itself inevitably into a caste, as soon as it conquers power. The history of the twentieth century has shown us time and again the inexorable transformation of revolutionary parties into pitiless bureaucracies. The phenomenon has repeated itself everywhere: dictatorship by the Communist Party of the society; dictatorship of the Central Committee over the Communist Party; dictatorship of the revolutionary Caesar over the Central Committee. The Caesar can be called Brezhnev, Mao, or Fidel: the process is the same.

The repressive Soviet system is an inverted image of the political system created by Lenin. The forced-labor camps, the police bureaucracy that administers them, the arrests without process of law, the judgments behind closed doors, the torture, the intimidation, the calumnies, the self-accusations and confessions, the general spying: all this is the consequence of the dictatorship of the sole Party and, within the Party of dictatorship, of one group and one man. The political pyramid that is the Communist system is reproduced in the inverted pyramid of their repressive system. In turn, the repression the Party exercises on the populace is reproduced in the heart of the Party itself: the elimination of external opposition is succeeded necessarily by the elimination of internal rivals and dissidents: the Bolsheviks followed the road of the Mensheviks, Anarchists, and Revolutionary Socialists. President Liu-Shao-Ch'i and his old enemy Marshal Lin Piao lie now together, mingled in the same historical opprobrium. Recourse to bloody purges and cultural revolutions is no accident: how else can the middle and upper echelons of Party directors be renewed, and how else could political disputes and rivalries be resolved? The suppression of internal democracy condemns the Party to violent periodic convulsions.

EVEN IF we think economic structures are governed by us, it is impossible to ignore the decisive function of ideologies in historical life. Though according to Marx and Engels ideologies are mere

117

superstructures, the truth is that these "superstructures" often outlive the "structures." Christianity outlived the bureaucratic and imperial regime of Constantine, medieval feudalism, the absolute monarchies of the seventeenth century, and the national bourgeois democracies of the nineteenth. Buddhism has revealed even greater vitality. And what of Confucianism? It will probably survive Mao, as it has survived the Han, the Tang, and the Ming. And, deeper than ideologies, there is another realm scarcely affected by historical change: beliefs. Magic and astrology, to call on two well-worn examples, have survived Plato and Aristotle, Abelard and Saint Thomas, Kant and Hegel, Nietzsche and Freud. Thus, to explain the repressive Soviet system we have to bear in mind various levels or strata of social and historical reality. For Trotsky, Stalinism was above all a consequence of the social and economic backwardness of Russia: the economic structure determined it. For other critics, it was rather the result of Bolshevik ideology. Both explanations are, at the same time, exact and incomplete. It seems to me that another factor is no less important: the very history of Russia, its religious and political tradition, all that half-conscious, airy element of beliefs, feelings, and images that constitutes what earlier historians called the *genius* (the soul) of society.

There is a clear continuity between the despotism exercised by Peter and Catherine and that of Lenin and Trotsky, between the bloodthirsty paranoia of Ivan the Terrible and Stalin. Stalinism and czarist autocracy were born, grew, and fed upon Russian reality. The same must be said of the bureaucracy and the police system. Autocracy and bureaucracy are features which Russia probably inherited from Byzantium, along with Christianity and the great art. Other features in Russian society are Oriental, and others have their origin in Slavic paganism. The history of Russia is a strange mixture of sensuality and exalted spiritualism, brutality and heroism, saintliness and abject superstition. Russian "primitivism" has been described or analyzed many times, now with admiration and now with horror. It is, one must confess, a very unprimitive primitivism: not only did it create one of the most profound, rich, and complex literatures in the world, but it also represents a living and unique spiritual tradition of our time. I am convinced that that tradition is called to give life, like a spring, to the drought, the egoism, and the decay of the contemporary West. The stories told by the survivors of the Nazi and the Soviet concentration camps reveal the difference between Western "modernity" and Russian "primitivism." In the case of the former, the words ceaselessly repeated are *inhumanity, impersonality*, and *homicidal efficiency*; while in the case of the latter, besides the horror and bestiality, words like *compassion, charity*, and *fraternity* stand out. The Russian nation has preserved, as one can see from the contemporary writers and intellectuals, a Christian foundation.

Russia is not primitive: it is *ancient*. Despite the Revolution, its modernity is incomplete: Russia did not have an eighteenth century. It would be useless to seek in its intellectual, philosophical, or moral tradition a Hume, a Kant, or a Diderot. This explains, at least in part, the coexistence in modern Russia of precapitalist virtues and vices such as indifference to political and social liberties. There is a similarity—as yet little explored—between the Spanish and the Russian traditions: neither they nor we, the Latin Americans, have a critical tradition because neither they nor we had in fact anything which can be compared with the Enlightenment and the intellectual movement of the eighteenth century in Europe. Nor did we have anything to compare with the Protestant Reformation, that great seedbed of liberties and democracy in the modern world. Thence the failure of the tentative democracies in Spain and its old colonies. The Spanish empire disintegrated and with it our countries too. Confronted with the anarchy which followed the dissolution of the Spanish order, we had no remedy but the barbaric remedy of tyranny. The sad contemporary reality is the result of the failure of our wars of independence: we were unable to rebuild, on modern principles, the Spanish order. Dismembered, each part became a victim of the chiefs of armed groups—our generals and presidents—and of imperialism, especially that of the United States. With independence, our countries did not begin a new phase: rather, the end of the Spanish world was hastened and achieved. When will we recover? In Russia there was no disintegration: the Communist bureaucracy replaced the czarist autocracy.

Like a good Russian, Solzhenitsyn would resign himself—he has said recently—to seeing his country ruled by a nondemocratic regime so long as it corresponded, however distantly, with the image that traditional thought created of the Christian sovereign, afraid of God and loving his subjects. An idea, I mention in passing, that has its equivalent in the "universal sovereign" of Buddhism (Asoka is the great example) and in the Confucian idea that the emperor rules by heavenly mandate. The Russian novelist's idea may seem fantastic, and to a certain degree it is. Nonetheless, it corresponds rather to a more realistic and deeper vision of the history of his country. And we, Spanish-Americans and Spaniards, is it not time that we examined more soberly and realistically our present and our past? When will we evolve our own political thought? A century and a half of petty tyrants, pronouncements, and military dictatorships—has this not opened our eyes? Our failure to adapt democratic institutions, in their two modern versions—the Anglo-Saxon and the French—ought to compel us to think on our own account, without looking through the spectacles of modish ideology. The contradiction between our institutions and what we really are is scandalous and would be comical were it not tragic. I feel no nostalgia for the Indian King or the Viceroy, for the Lady Serpent or the Grand Inquisitor, nor for His Most Serene Highness, or the Hero of Peace or the Great Chief of the Revolution. But these grotesque, frightening titles denote realities, and those realities are more real than our laws and constitutions. It is useless to close our eyes to them and more useless still to repress our past and condemn it to live on in history's subsoil; the life underground strengthens it, and periodically it reappears as a destructive eruption or explosion. This is the result of the ingenuity, hypocrisy, or stupidity of those who pretend to bury it alive. We need to *name* our past, to find political and juridical forms to integrate it and transform it into a creative force. Only thus will we begin to be free.

The system of sending delinquents against the common order along with political prisoners to Siberia was not a Communist but a czarist invention. The infamous Russian penal colonies were known throughout the world, and in 1886 an American explorer, George Kennan, devoted a book to this somber subject: *Siberia and the Exile System*. The reader need not be reminded of Dostoevski's *House of the Dead*. Less known is Anton Chekhov's *The Island, a Voyage to Sajalin*. But there is an essential difference: Dostoevski's and Chekhov's books were published legally in czarist Russia, while Solzhenitsyn had to publish his book abroad with the known risks. In 1890 Chekhov decided to travel to the celebrated penal colony of Sajalin and write a book on the Russian penitentiary system. Though it seems strange, the czarist authorities permitted his journey, and the Russian writer was able to interview the prisoners with considerable freedom (except for the political prisoners). Five years later, in 1895, he published his book, a complete condemnation of the Russian penal system. Chekhov's experience under czarism is unthinkable in any twentieth-century Marxist-Leninist regime.

As well as the circumstances of historical and national organizations, the place of individuals in the general order must be mentioned. Almost always these orders are interwoven with international realities and the national context. For example, in the case of Yugoslavia, Tito, as well as being the head of the Communist Party, led the nationalist resistance first against the Nazis

121

and afterward against Stalin's attempts at intervention. Yugoslav nationalism contributed to the regime's relaxation of the terrible burden of the Russian and Leninist tradition: Yugoslavia humanized itself. It would be an error to ignore the beneficent influence of Tito's personality in that revolution. In each of the Communist states the Caesar imposes his style on the regime. In the time of Stalin, the color of the system was the rabid yellow and green of rage; today it is gray like Brezhnev's conscience. In China the regime is no less oppressive than in Russia, but its customs are not brutal or glacial: no Ivan the Terrible but Huang Ti, the first emperor. There is a striking resemblance between Huang and Mao, as Etiemble pointed out (see *Plural* 29, February 1974). Both rivals of Confucius and both possessed by the same superhuman ambition: to make time itself—past, present, and future—a huge monument that repeats its features. Time becomes malleable, history is a docile substance which takes on the kind and terrible imprint of the president-emperor. The first Cultural Revolution was the burning of the Chinese classics, especially the books of Confucius, ordered by Huang Ti in 213 B.C. Local variations on a universal archetype: the Caesar of Havana makes use of dialectics much as the old Spanish landowners used the whip.

THE SIMILARITIES between the Stalinist and Nazi regimes make it right for us to describe them both as totalitarian. That is the point of view of Hannah Arendt, but also of a man like Andrei Sakharov, one of the fathers of the Russian H-bomb:

> Nazism survived for twelve years; Stalinism twice as long. Besides the various common features, there are differences between them. The hypocrisy and demagogy of Stalin were of a more subtle order, depending not on a frankly barbarous program like Hitler's but on a socialist ideology, a progressive,

scientific, and popular ideology which was a useful screen to deceive the working class, and to anesthetize the vigilance of the intellectuals and of rivals in the struggle for power. . . . Thanks to that "peculiarity" of Stalinism, the most terrible blows were delivered to the Soviet people and their most active, competent and honorable representatives. Between ten and fifteen million Soviet citizens, at least, have perished in the dungeons of the NKVD, martyred or executed, and in the camps for "Kulaks" and their families, camps "without right of correspondence" (those camps were the prototypes for the Nazi extermination camps), or dead of cold and hunger or exhausted by the inhuman labor in the glacial mines of Norilsk and Vorkuta, in the countless quarries and forest exploitations, in the construction of canals or, simply, from being transported in closed train cars or drowned in the "ships of death" on the Sea of Okhotsk, during the deportation of whole populations, the Tartars from Crimea, the Germans from the Volga, Calmuks and other groups from the Caucasus. (*La liberté intellectuelle en URSS et la Coexistence*, Paris, Gallimard, 1968)

The testimony of the celebrated Soviet economist Eugene Varga is no less impressive:

Though in Stalin's dungeons and concentration camps there were fewer cruel men and sadists than in Hitler's camps, it can be affirmed that no difference in principle existed between them. Many of those executioners are still at liberty and receive comfortable pensions. (*Testament*, 1964: Paris, Granet, 1970)

However terrible the testimony of Solzhenitsyn, Sakharov, Varga, and many others, it seems to me that a crucial distinction ought to be made: neither the pre-Stalin period (1918–1928) nor the post-Stalin period (1956–1974) can be compared with nazism. Therefore one must distinguish, as Hannah Arendt does, between totalitarian systems properly speaking (nazism and Stalinism) and

123

Communist bureaucratic dictatorships. Nevertheless it is clear that there is a causal relationship between Bolshevism and totalitarianism: without the dictatorship of the Party over the country and the Central Committee over the Party, Stalinism could not have developed. Trotsky thought the difference between communism and nazism consisted in the different organization of the economy: state property in the former and capitalist property in the latter. The truth is that, beyond the differences in the control of property, the two systems are similar in being bureaucratic dictatorships of one group which stands above class, society, and morality. The notion of a separate group is crucial. That group is a political party which initially takes the form of a gathering of conspirators. When it takes power, the conspirators' secret cell becomes the police cell, equally secret, for interrogation and torture. Leninism is not Stalinism but one of its antecedents. The others are in the Russian past, as well as in human nature.

Beyond Leninism is Marxism. I allude to the original Marxism, worked out by Marx and Engels in their mature years. That Marxism too contains the germs of authoritarianism—though to a far lesser degree than in Lenin and Trotsky—and many of the criticisms Bakunin leveled at it are still valid. But the germs of liberty which are found in the writings of Marx and Engels are no less fertile and powerful than the dogmatic Hegelian inheritance. And another thing: the socialist program is essentially a Promethean program of liberation of men and nations. Only from this point of view can (and ought) a criticism of the authoritarian tendencies in Marxism be made. In 1956 Bertrand Russell admirably summarized the stance of a free spirit confronting terrorist dogmas:

> My objections to modern Communism are far deeper than my objections to Marx. What I find particularly disastrous is the abandonment of democracy. A minority which leans for support on the activities of the secret police must necessarily be-

come a cruel, oppressive and obscurantist minority. The dangers which irresponsible power engenders were generally recognized during the eighteenth and nineteenth centuries, but many, blinded by the external successes of the Soviet Union, have forgotten all that which was painfully learned during the years of absolute monarchy: victims of the curious illusion that they form part of the vanguard of progress, they have reverted to the worst periods of the Middle Ages. (*Portraits from Memory*, New York, 1956)

The rejection of Caesarism and of Communist dictatorship does not in any way imply a justification of American imperialism, of racism, or of the atomic bomb; nor a shutting of the eyes before the injustice of the capitalist system. We cannot justify what happens in the West and in Latin America by saying that what happens in Russia and Czechoslovakia is worse: horrors there do not justify horrors here. What happens among us is unjustifiable, whether it is the prison detention of Onetti, the murders in Chile, or the tortures in Brazil. But nor is it possible for us to be blind to the misfortunes of the Russian, Czech, Chinese, or Cuban dissidents. The defense of so-called formal liberties is, day by day, the first political duty of a writer, whether in Mexico, in Moscow, or in Montevideo. The "formal liberties" are not, of course, all liberty, and liberty itself is not the sole human aspiration: fraternity, justice, equality, and security are also desirable. But without those formal liberties—of thought, expression, of association and movement, of saying "no" to power—there is no fraternity, no justice, nor hope of equality.

On this we ought to be unswerving and denounce implacably all equivocations, confusions, and lies. It is inadmissible, for example, that people who even a few months ago were calling the freedom of the press a "bourgeois trick" and were encouraging students, in the name of a radicalism both hackneyed and obscurantist, to violate the principle of academic freedom now form

125

committees and sign manifestos to defend that very freedom of the press in Uruguay and Chile. Recently Günter Grass was putting us on our guard, recalling the pseudoradical frivolity of German intellectuals in the period of the Weimar Republic. While there was democracy in Germany, they never ceased to scoff at it as an illusion and a bourgeois plot, but when, fatally, Hitler came, they fled—not to Moscow but to New York, doubtless to pursue there with increased ardor their critique of bourgeois society.

The moral and structural similarities between Stalinism and nazism should not make us forget their distinct ideological origins. Nazism was a narrowly nationalist and racist ideology, while Stalinism was a perversion of the great and beautiful socialist tradition. Leninism presents itself as a universal doctrine. It is impossible to be unmoved by the Lenin of *The State and Revolution*. Equally, it is impossible to forget that he was the founder of the Cheka and the man who unleashed terror against the Mensheviks and Revolutionary Socialists, his comrades in arms. Almost all Western and Latin American writers, at one point or another in our lives, sometimes because of generous but ignorant impulses, sometimes out of weakness under the pressure of the intellectual milieu, and sometimes simply to be modish, have allowed ourselves to be seduced by Leninism. When I consider Aragon, Eluard, Neruda, and other famous Stalinist writers and poets, I feel the gooseflesh that I get from reading certain passages in the *Inferno*. No doubt they began in good faith. How could they have shut their eyes to the horrors of capitalism and the disasters of imperialism in Asia, Africa, and our part of America? They experienced a generous surge of indignation and of solidarity with the victims. But insensibly, commitment by commitment, they saw themselves become tangled in a mesh of lies, falsehoods, deceits, and perjuries, until they lost their souls. They became, literally, soulless. This may seem exaggerated: Dante and his punishments for some wrongheaded political views? Who nowadays anyway believes in the soul? I will add that our opinions on this subject have not been mere errors or flaws in our faculty of judgment. They have been a sin in the old religious sense of that word: something that affects the whole being. Very few of us could look a Solzhenitsyn, or a Nadejda Mandelstam, in the eye. That sin has stained us and, fatally, has stained our writings as well. I say this with sadness, and with humility.

Mexico, March 1974

GULAG:
BETWEEN ISAIAH
AND JOB*

Some writers and journalists, in Mexico and elsewhere in America and Europe, have criticized with a certain harshness things— some of them admittedly far of the mark—that Solzhenitsyn has said in recent months. The tone of these recriminations, ranging from the vindictive to the relieved "I told you so," is that of the man who has had a weight lifted from his shoulders: "Ah, that explains it all, Solzhenitsyn is a reactionary. . . ." This attitude is another indication that the attacks against the revelations about the totalitarian Soviet system which the writer has made were

---

*This essay was published twenty months after Paz's first essay on Solzhenitsyn. It extends some of the arguments advanced in that piece and distinguishes between Solzhenitsyn the witness and Solzhenitsyn the social theorist.

128

accepted *à contre coeur* by many Western and Latin American intellectuals. It's hardly surprising: the Bolshevik myth, the faith in the essential purity and goodwill of the Soviet Union, above and beyond its failures and errors, is a superstition not easily eradicated. The ancient theological distinction between *substance* and *accident* continues to serve our century's believers with the same efficacy that it did in the Middle Ages: the substance is Marxism-Leninism and the accident is Stalinism. That's why, when Solzhenitsyn's early books were published, the brilliant, casuistical Lukács tried to turn their author into a "socialist realist," that is, a dissident *within* the Church. But Solzhenitsyn's emergence—not only his, but the appearance of many other independent Russian writers and intellectuals—was and is significant for precisely the opposite reason: they are dissidents outside the Church. Their repudiation of Marxism-Leninism is complete. This is what seems to me portentous: more than half a century after the October Revolution, many Russian spirits, perhaps the best—scientists, novelists, historians, poets, and philosophers— have ceased to be Marxists. A few have even returned—like Solzhenitsyn and Brodsky—to Christianity. It is a phenomenon incomprehensible to many European and American intellectuals. Incomprehensible and unacceptable.

I don't know if history repeats itself: I know that men change very little. There is no salvation outside the Church. If Solzhenitsyn is not a dissident revolutionary, he must be a reactionary imperialist. To condemn Solzhenitsyn, who dared to speak, is to absolve oneself—a self that has preserved its silence for years and years. The truth is that Solzhenitsyn is neither a revolutionary nor a reactionary: his is another tradition. When he repudiated Marxism-Leninism he repudiated too the "enlightened" and progressivist tradition of the West. He is as far from Kant and Robespierre as he is from Marx and Lenin. Nor does he feel drawn to Adam Smith or Jefferson. He is not liberal, not democrat, not capitalist. He believes in liberty—yes—because he believes in human dignity; he also believes in charity and comradeship, not in representative democracy nor in class solidarity. He would accept a Russia ruled by an autocrat, providing that autocrat were at the same time a genuine Christian: someone who believed in the sanctity of the human being, in the daily mystery of the other, who is our fellow creature. Here I ought to pause briefly to say that I disagree with Solzhenitsyn in this: Christians do not love their fellow creatures. And they do not love them because they have never *really* believed in otherness. History shows us how when they have found it they have converted it or destroyed it. At the root of Christians, as at the root of their descendants the Marxists, I perceive a terrible self-disgust which makes them hate and envy others, especially if those others are pagans. This is the psychological source of their missionary zeal and of the Inquisitions with which now one faction, now another, have darkened the planet.

Solzhenitsyn's Christianity is not dogmatic or inquisitorial. If his faith distances him from the political institutions created by the bourgeois revolution, it also makes him an enemy to the idolatry of Caesar and his embalmed corpse, and to the fanatic adherence to the letter of "holy writ," those two religions of Communist states. In short, Solzhenitsyn's world is a premodern society with its system of special laws, local liberties, and individual privileges of exemption. Yet, archaic though his political philosophy seems to us, his vision reflects with greater clarity than the critiques of his detractors the historical crossroads at which we find ourselves. I admit that often his line of reasoning fails to convince me and that his intellectual style is alien and contrary to my mental habits, my aesthetic tastes, and indeed my moral convictions. I am nearer to Celsius than to Saint Paul, I prefer Plotinus to Saint Augustine and Hume to Pascal. But Solzhenitsyn's direct and simple vision penetrates actuality and reveals to us what is hidden in the folds and creases of our days. Moral passion is a passion for truth and it provokes the appearance of truth. There is a prophetic element in his writings which I do not find in the work of any other of my contemporaries. Sometimes, as in Dante's tercets—though the Russian's prose is ponderous and his arguments prolix—I hear the voice of Isaiah and I recoil and rebel; at other times, I hear the voice of Job and I pity and accept. Like the prophets and like Dante, the Russian writer tells us of actuality from the other shore, that shore I dare not call eternal because I do not believe in eternity. Solzhenitsyn tells us what is happening, what is happening to us, what is violating us. He treats history from the double perspective of the now and the forever.

Apart from certain countries whose histories are separate from the general history of Europe toward the end of the seventeenth century (I'm thinking of Spain, Portugal, and the old American colonies of both nations), the West is living out the end of something which began at the close of the eighteenth century: that *modernity* which, in the political sphere, found expression in representative democracy, balance of power, the equality of citizens before the law, and the system of human rights and individual guarantees. As if it were an ironic and devilish confirmation of Marx's predictions—a confirmation in reverse—bourgeois democracy dies at the hands of its own historical creation. Thus Hegel's and his disciples' creative negation seems to fulfill itself in a perverse way: the infant matricide, destroyer of the old order, is not the universal proletariat but the new Leviathan, the bureaucratic state. Revolution destroys the bourgeoisie but not to liberate men—rather to enchain them more cruelly. The connection between the bureaucratic state and the industrial system, created by bourgeois democracy, is so close that a critique of the first implies necessarily a critique of the second.

MARXISM IS INADEQUATE IN OUR TIME because its critique of capitalism, far from including industrialism, includes an apology for its works. To laud technology and believe in industry as the greatest liberating agent of man—a belief common to capitalists and Communists—was logical in 1850, legitimate in 1900, understandable in 1920, but it is scandalous in 1975. Today we are aware that the evil is implicit not solely in the system of ownership of the means of production, but in the means of production themselves. Naturally it is impossible to renounce industry; it's not impossible to stop making a god of it, or to limit its destructiveness. Apart from the noxious ecological consequences, perhaps irreparable, the industrial system includes social dangers which no one now can be blind to. It is inhuman and dehumanizes all that it touches, from the "lords of the machines" to their "servants," as the economist Perroux calls those involved in the process: owners, technocrats, and workers. Whatever the political regime in which it evolves, modern industry automatically generates impersonal structures of labor and human relations no less impersonal, pitiless, and mechanical. Those structures and those relations contain a power, like the germ of the future organism, the bureaucratic state with its administrators, its moralists, its judges and psychiatrists and camps for labor reeducation.

Ever since it first appeared, Marxism has pretended to know the secret of the laws of historical evolution. It has not, throughout its history, abandoned this pretense and it is found in the writings of all the sects into which it has split, from Bernstein to Kautsky and from Lenin to Mao. Nonetheless, among its prophecies for the future there is no mention of the possibility which now seems to us most threatening and imminent: bureaucratic totalitarianism as the unraveling of the crisis of bourgeois society. There is one exception: Leon Trotsky. I mention him—though one swallow doesn't make a summer—because his case is full of pathos. At the end of his life, in the last article he wrote, shortly before he was murdered, Trotsky evoked—without much faith in it, just in passing, as one who shakes off a nightmare—the hypothesis that the Marxist view of modern history as the final triumph of socialism might be a hideous error of perspective. Then he said that, in view of the absence of proletarian revolutions in the West, during the Second World War or immediately after it the crisis of capitalism would resolve itself in the appearance of totalitarian collectivist societies whose earliest historical realizations were, in those days (1939), Hitler's Germany and Stalin's Russia. Since then, some Trotskyite groups (though dissidents within that movement, like those that publish *Socialisme ou Barbarie*) have directed their analysis into the area indicated by Trotsky, but they have not managed to devise a genuinely Marxist theory of totalitarian collectivism. The main obstacle in the way of a clear understanding of the phenomenon is their failure to recognize, as their teacher had, the class nature of the bureaucracy.*

Oddly, the only thing Trotsky thought of to confront the new Leviathan was—to elaborate a minimal program of defense of the workers! It's revealing that, despite his extraordinary intelligence, he did not consider two circumstances. The first is that he, with his dogmatic intolerance and his rigid conception of the Bolshevik Party as the instrument of history, had contributed powerfully to the construction of the world's first bureaucratic state. That irony is the more wounding if we remember that Lenin, in his Will, reproaches Trotsky for his bureaucratic leanings and his tendency to treat problems from the purely administrative angle. The second circumstance is the disproportion between the magnitude of the evil Trotsky perceived—a totalitarian collectivism instead of socialism—and the inanity of the remedy: a minimal plan of action. A curious vision of professional revo-

---

*I was too sweeping. We owe to Cornelius Costariadis and to Claude Lefort valuable and illuminating analyses of the historical nature of the Russian bureaucratic State that vastly overcome the limitations of the traditional Trotskyite critique. See my book *One Earth, Four or Five Worlds* (1985).

lutionaries: they reduce the history of the world to the editing of a manifesto and the forming of committees. Bureaucracy and apocalypse.

The bureaucratic state is not exclusively found in countries called socialist. It happened in Germany and it could happen elsewhere: industrial society carries it in its womb. The great multinational companies prefigure it, as do other institutions that form a part of Western democracies, like the American CIA. Nonetheless, if liberty is to survive the bureaucratic state, it ought to find a different alternative to the ones that capitalist democracies offer today. The weakness of these democracies is not physical but spiritual. They are richer and more powerful than their totalitarian adversaries, but they do not know what to do with their power and their wealth. Without faith in anything beyond immediate profit, they have time and time again entered into pacts with crime. This is what Solzhenitsyn has said—though in the religious language of another age—and this is what has scandalized the Pharisees. I'll add something I should have said before: Western democracies have protected and continue to protect all the tyrants and petty tyrants of the five continents.

It's often said that Solzhenitsyn has revealed nothing new. That is true: we all knew that in the Soviet Union forced-labor camps existed and that they were extermination camps for millions of human beings. What is new is that the majority of "left-wing intellectuals" has at last accepted that the paradise was in fact hell. This return to reason, I fear, is due not so much to Solzhenitsyn's genius as to the salutary effects of Khrushchev's revelations. They believed as they were told and they ceased to believe as they were told. Perhaps for this reason few—very few—of them have had the humble courage to analyze in public what went wrong and to explain the reasons that moved them to think and act as they did. The reluctance to admit error is such that one of those hardened souls, a great poet, said: "How could I, a writer, have avoided erring, when History itself erred?" The Greeks and the Aztecs knew that their gods sinned, but modern men surpass the ancients: History, that fleshed-out idea, like a scatterbrained matron goes on a spree with the first comer, whether his name is Tamburlaine or Stalin. This is where Marxism has come to rest, a system of thought that presents itself as "the critique of heaven."

In an article I wrote on the publication of the first volume of *The Gulag Archipelago*, I emphasized that the respect Solzhenitsyn inspires in me does not imply adherence to his ideas or to his stance. I approve his criticism of the Soviet regime and of the hedonism, hypocrisy, and myopic opportunism of the Western democracies; I repudiate his simplistic idea of history as a battle between two empires and two trends. Solzhenitsyn has not understood that the century of the disintegration and liquidation of the European imperial system has also been the century of the rebirth of the old Asiatic nations, such as China, and the rise of young countries in Africa and elsewhere in the world. Will those movements resolve themselves in a gigantic historical failure like the failure, up to now, of Brazil and the Spanish American nations, born a century and a half ago out of the Spanish and Portuguese disintegration? It is impossible to know, but the case of China seems to point in the other direction.

Solzhenitsyn's ignorance is serious because its true name is arrogance. It is, above all, a very Russian trait, as anyone who has had dealings with writers and intellectuals from that country, whether dissident or orthodox, knows. This is another of the great Russian mysteries, as all readers of Dostoevski know: in Russians arrogance goes hand in hand with humility, brutality with piety, fanaticism with the greatest spiritual liberty. The insensibility and blindness of a great writer and a great heart: Solzhenitsyn the brave and the pious has revealed a certain *imperial* indifference, in the ample sense of the word, in the face of the sufferings of peoples humiliated and subjected by the West.

135

The strangest thing of all is that, being as he is a friend and witness to liberty, he should not have felt sympathy with the struggles of those peoples for freedom.

THE CASE OF VIETNAM illustrates Solzhenitsyn's limitations. His and his critics'. Those groups who opposed, almost always with good and legitimate reasons, the American intervention in Indochina denied at the same time something undeniable: the conflict was an episode in the battle between Washington and Moscow. Not to see it—or to try not to see it—was to be blind to what Solzhenitsyn and (also) Mao saw: the defeat of the Americans encourages the aspirations toward Soviet hegemony in Asia and Eastern Europe. Those same groups—socialists, libertarians, democrats, anti-imperialist liberals—denounced justifiably the immorality and corruption of the South Vietnamese regime but did not say a single word about the actual nature of the one that ruled in North Vietnam. A witness beyond suspicion, Jean Lacouture, has called the Hanoi government the most Stalinist in the Communist world. Its leader, Ho Chi Minh, directed a bloody purge against Trotskyites and other dissidents of the left when he took power. The cruel measures adopted by the triumvirate which rules Cambodia have shocked and shamed Western supporters of the Khmer Rouge. All this proves that the left is snared in its own ideology; that is why it has not yet found the means of combating imperialism without succoring totalitarianism instead. But Solzhenitsyn himself is a victim of the ideological snare: he said that the war in Indochina was an imperial conflict, but he did not say that it was also—and above all else—a war of national liberation. This was what legitimized it. To ignore this fact is to ignore not only the complexity of all historical reality but also its human and moral dimension. Manichaeism is the moralist's trap.

Solzhenitsyn's opinions do not invalidate his testimony. *The*

Gulag Archipelago is neither a book of political philosophy nor a sociological treatise. Its theme is something else: human suffering in its two most extreme aspects, abjection and heroism. It is not the suffering which nature or destiny or the gods inflict, but which man inflicts on his fellow man. The theme is as ancient as human society, ancient as the primitive hordes and as Cain. It is a political, biological, psychological, philosophical, and religious theme: evil. No one has yet been able to tell us why evil exists in the world and why evil abides in man. Solzhenitsyn's work has two virtues, both great: first, it is the account of something lived and suffered; second, it constitutes a complete and horrifying encyclopedia of political horror in the twentieth century. The two volumes which have appeared so far are a geography and an anatomy of the *evil* of our era. That evil is not melancholy or despair or *taedium vitae* but sadism without an erotic element: crime socialized and submitted to the norms of mass production. A crime monotonous as an infinite multiplication exercise. What age and what civilization can offer a book to compare with Solzhenitsyn's or with the accounts of the survivors of the Nazi camps? Our civilization has touched the extreme of evil (Hitler, Stalin), and those books reveal it. This is the root of their greatness. The resistance which Solzhenitsyn's books have provoked is explicable: those books are the evocation of a reality whose very existence is the most thorough refutation, desolating and convincing, of several centuries of utopian thought, from Campanella to Fourier and from More to Marx. Moreover, they are a life study of a loathsome society but one in which millions of our contemporaries—among them countless writers, scientists, artists—have seen nothing less than the adorable features of the Best of Future Worlds. What do they say to themselves now, if they dare to speak to themselves, the authors of those exalted travelogues to the USSR (one of them was called *Return from the Future*), those enthusiastic poems and those impassioned reports about "the fatherland of socialism"?

The Gulag Archipelago takes the double form of a history and a catalogue. The history of the origin, development, and proliferation of a cancer which began as a *tactical* measure at a difficult stage in the struggle for power and which ended as a social *institution* in whose destructive function millions of human beings participated, some as victims and others as executioners, guards, and accomplices. The catalogue: an inventory of the gradations—gradations also in the scale of being—between bestiality and saintliness. In telling us of the birth, the development, and the transformation of the totalitarian cancer, Solzhenitsyn writes a chapter, perhaps the most terrible chapter, in the general history of the collective Cain; in telling us the cases he has witnessed and those which other eyewitnesses have told him—witnesses in the evangelical sense of the word—he gives us a vision of man. The history is social; the catalogue individual. The history is limited: social systems are born, evolve, and die; they're ephemeral. The catalogue is not historical: it relates not to the system but to the human condition. Abjection and its complement: the vision of Job on his dungheap has no term.

Mexico, December 1975

JOSÉ ORTEGA Y GASSET: THE WHY AND THE WHEREFORE*

I write these lines with enthusiasm and with fear. Enthusiasm because I always admired José Ortega y Gasset; fear because— apart from my personal inadequacies—I do not believe one can summarize or judge in an essay a literary and philosophical oeuvre as vast and varied as his. A philosophy which can be summarized in a phrase is not a philosophy but a religion. Or its counterfeit: ideology. Buddhism is the most intellectual and discursive of religions; all the same, a sutra condenses the entire doctrine in the monosyllable *a*, the particle of universal negation. Christianity, too, can be stated in one or two phrases, such as "Love

*This essay first appeared in a special issue of the Madrid daily paper *El País* dedicated to the memory of José Ortega y Gasset on the twenty-fifth anniversary of his death.

139

one another" or "My kingdom is not of this world." The same thing happens, at a lower level, with ideologies. For example: "Universal history is the history of the war of the classes" or, in the liberal camp, "Progress is the law of societies." The difference is that ideologies pretend to talk in the name of science. As Alain Besançon says: the religious man *knows that he believes* while the ideologue *believes that he knows* (Tertullian and Lenin). Maxims, tags, the sayings, and the articles of faith do not impoverish religion: they are seeds which grow and fruit in the heart of the faithful. Philosophy, by contrast, is nothing if not development, demonstration, and justification of an idea or an intuition. Without explication there is no philosophy. Nor, of course, criticism of the philosophical work.

To the difficulty of reducing to a few pages so rich and complex a body of thought as Ortega y Gasset's, one must add the actual character of his writings. He was a true essayist, perhaps the greatest in the Spanish language; that is, he was a master of a genre which does not allow the simplifications of synopsis. The essayist must be diverse, penetrating, acute, fresh, and he must master the difficult art of using three dots . . . He does not exhaust his theme, he neither compiles nor systematizes: he explores. If he succumbs to the temptation to be categorical, as Ortega y Gasset so often did, he should introduce into what he says a few drops of doubt, a reserve. The prose of the essay flows in a lively way, never in a straight line, but always equidistant from the two extremes which ceaselessly lie in wait for it: the treatise and the aphorism. Two forms of freezing.

Like a good essayist, Ortega y Gasset came back from each of his expeditions through unknown lands with unusual discoveries and trophies but without having charted a map of the new land. He did not colonize: he discovered. This is why I have never understood the complaint of those who say he left us no complete books (that is, treatises, systems). Can one not say the same of

Montaigne and of Thomas Browne, of Renan and of Carlyle? The essays of Schopenhauer are not inferior to his great philosophical work. The same thing happens, in our century, with Bertrand Russell. Wittgenstein himself, author of the most rigorous and geometrical book of philosophy of modern times, felt after writing it the need to write books more like the essay, acts of unsystematic reflection and meditation. It was fortunate that Ortega y Gasset did not succumb to the temptation of the treatise or the summa. His genius did not predispose him to define or to construct. He was neither a geometrician nor an architect. I see his works not as a collection of buildings but as a net of roads and navigable rivers. An oeuvre to be traveled through rather than resided in: he invites us not to stay but to move on.

He touched on an astonishing diversity of themes. More astonishing is how frequently those various subjects resolve themselves in genuine discoveries. Much of what he said is still worth remembering and discussing. I have already mentioned the extraordinary mobility of his thought: to read him is to walk briskly along difficult byways toward hardly glimpsed goals; sometimes one reaches the destination and sometimes one remains on the outskirts. No matter: what is important is the making of trails. But to read him is also to linger before this or that idea, to put the book aside and risk thinking on one's own account. His prose marshals verbs such as *incite, instigate, provoke, goad*. Some have reproached him for certain harshnesses and arrogances. Though I, too, lament those acrimonies, I understand that our countries— always drowsy, especially when they are possessed, as they now are, by violent agitations—need those goadings and stabs. Others criticize him because he did not know how to speak quietly. That is also true. I still ask myself how to resist raising one's voice in countries that are violent and lethargic? I add that his best writings, above and beyond the stimulus they give us, also give us illumination. They are something unusual in Spanish: exercises in clarity which are also attempts at clarification. That was one of his great gifts to Spanish prose: he showed that clarity was a form of intellectual cleanliness.

His essays on—I don't know whether to call it social psychology or history of the collective soul—the discrimination between ideas and beliefs or between the revolutionary and the traditional spirit, his reflections on the evolution of love in the West and on fashion, the feminine and the masculine, age and youth, vital and historical rhythms—make one think more of Montaigne than of Kant and more of Stendhal than of Freud. He was a philosopher with the gift to penetrate deeply into the human. This gift was not that of a professional psychologist but of the novelist and historian, who see men not as solitary entities or isolated cases but as parts of a world. For the novelist and historian every man is already a society in himself. Though we are in Ortega y Gasset's debt for memorable essays on historical themes, it is sad that it never occurred to him, as it did to Hume, to write a history of his country. *Invertebrate Spain* would have been an admirable and memorable beginning for it: why did he not continue? It is also revealing that he did not use his powers of psychological divining to see himself. He was not an introvert and I do not imagine him writing a diary. There is something that I miss in his work: confession. Especially oblique confession, in the manner of Sterne. Perhaps the passion he felt for his circumstances—his great discovery and the axis of his thought—kept him from seeing himself.

His idea of the "I" was historical. Not the "I" of the contemplative, who has shut the door on the world, but of the man in relationship—it would be more just to say, in combat—with things and with other men. The world, as he explained many times, is inseparable from the "I." The unity or nucleus of the human being is an indissoluble relationship: the "I" is time and space; or: society, history—action. Thus it is not odd that among his best essays there are some on historical and political themes, such as *The Revolt of the Masses*, *The Theme of Our Time*, *The End of Revolutions* (full of extraordinary prophecies of what is happening today, though clouded by a cyclic idea of history which did not let him see completely the *unique* character of the revolutionary myth), *Man the Technician*, and so many others. Ortega y Gasset had, like Tocqueville, the highly rational ability to see what was coming. His lucidity contrasts with the blindness of so many of our prophets. If one compares his essays on contemporary historical and political themes with those of Sartre, one immediately perceives that he was more lucid and penetrating than the French philosopher. He was less often wrong, was more consistent, and thus saved himself (and us) all those rectifications which mar the work of Sartre and which ended with the late *mea culpa* of his last days. Comparison with Bertrand Russell, too, is not disadvantageous to Ortega y Gasset: the history of his political opinions, without being entirely coherent, does not abound in the contradictions and pirouettes of Russell's, who went from one extreme to the other. One can approve or reprove his political ideas, but one cannot accuse him—as one can the others—of inconsistency.

I may have been unfaithful to the tenor of his work in speaking of his *thought*. One ought rather to say, his *thoughts*. The plural is justified not because his thinking lacks unity but because it deals with a coherence inimical to system and which cannot be reduced to a chain of reasons and propositions. Despite the variety of the matter he dealt with, he did not leave us a dispersed oeuvre. On the contrary. But his genius was not interested in the form of theory, in the proper sense of the word, nor in the form of demonstration. He sometimes used the word *meditation*. It is exact, but *essay* is more general. Better said: *essays*, because the genre does not admit the singular. Though the unity of these essays is, clearly, of an intellectual order, their root is vital and even, I dare say, aesthetic. There is a way of thinking, a *style*, which is Ortega y Gasset's alone. In this method of operation

143

which combines intellectual rigor with the aesthetic necessity of personal expression lies the secret of his work's unity. Ortega y Gasset not only thought about this and that but also, from his earliest writings, decided that those thoughts, even those he took from his teachers and from the tradition, would bear his hallmark. To think was, for him, synonymous with expression. This was the opposite of Spinoza, who wanted to see his discourse, purged of impurities and accidents of the "I," as the verbal crystallization of mathematics, of the universal order. In this Ortega y Gasset was not far from the father of the essay, Montaigne. Many of Montaigne's ideas are drawn from antiquity and from some of his contemporaries, but his indisputable originality is not in the reading of Sextus Empiricus but in the way in which he lived and relived those ideas and how, in rethinking them, he changed them, made them his own and, thus, made them ours.

The number of ideas—what are called *ideas*—is not infinite. Philosophical speculation, for the last two and a half thousand years, has consisted of variations and combinations of concepts such as movement and identity, substance and change, being and entities, the one and the many, first principles and nothingness, etc. Naturally, those variations have been logically, vitally, and historically *necessary*. In the case of Ortega y Gasset this rethinking of the philosophical tradition and the thought of his age culminated in a question about the *why* and *how* of ideas. He inserted them into human life: thus they changed their nature, they were not essences which we contemplate in an unmoving heaven but instruments, weapons, mental objects which we use and live. Ideas are the forms of universal coexistence. He took the questioning of ideas further, to investigate what underlies and perhaps determines them: not the principle of sufficient reason but the domination of inarticulate beliefs. It is an hypothesis which, in another form, has reappeared in our days: the *beliefs* of Ortega y Gasset are, for Georges Dumézil, psychic structures, elemental in a society, present in its language and in its conception of the other world and of itself. The explanation for the immense influence Ortega y Gasset had on the intellectual life of our countries lies, no doubt, in this notion he had of ideas and concepts as *whys* and *hows*. They ceased to be entities beyond us and became vital spaces. His teaching consisted of showing us what ideas were for and how we could use them: not to know ourselves nor to contemplate essences but to open for ourselves a passage in our given circumstances, to converse with our world, with our past and with our kin.

Discourse with Ortega y Gasset was often a monologue. Many have regretted this, with some reason. Still, one must grant that that monologue taught us to think and made us talk, if not with ourselves, then with our Latin American history. He taught us that landscape is not a state of the soul and that we are not mere accidents of the landscape. The relationship between man and his environment is more complex than the antique relationship between subject and object. The environment is a "here" seen and lived from a "me"; that *from a me* is always a *from here*. The relation between one pole and another is, more than a dialogue, an interaction. Ideas are reactions, acts. This view, at once erotic and polemic of human destiny, does not open into any beyond. There is no transcendence beyond the act or the thought which, when it is carried out, is exhausted: then, under threat of extinction, one must begin again. Man is a being who continually makes and remakes himself. The great invention of man is men.

This is a Promethean and also a tragic view: if we are a perpetual self-creation, we are an eternal rebeginning. There is no rest: end and beginning are the same. And there is no human nature: man is not a given but something that makes and discovers itself. From the beginning of the beginning, cast out of himself and out of nature, he is a being in the air; all his creations— what we call culture and history—are nothing more than contrivances to keep him suspended in the air so that he will not fall back into the bestial inertia that preceded the beginning. History

145

is our condition and our liberty: it is what we are in and what we make. Yet history does not consist of settled accounts, but of a suspension in the air, rootless, outside nature. I have always been staggered by this vision of man as a creature in permanent struggle against the laws of gravity. But it is a vision in which the other face of reality does not appear: history as an incessant production of ruins, man as fall and continual self-unmaking. I fear Ortega y Gasset's philosophy lacked the weight, the gravity, of death. There are two great absences in his work: Epictetus and Saint Augustine.

His intellectual endeavor found three outlets: his books, his teaching, and the *Revista de Occidente* with its publishing list. His influence left a deep mark on the cultural life of Spain and Latin America. For the first time, after a two-century eclipse, Spanish thought was heard and discussed in Latin American countries. Not only were our ways of thought and our funds of information renewed and changed; literature, the arts, and the sensibility of the age also show the marks of Ortega y Gasset and his circle. Between 1920 and 1935 in the enlightened classes, as they were called in the nineteenth century, a *style* predominated which came from the *Revista de Occidente*. I am sure that Ortega's thought will be discovered, and very soon, by younger Spanish generations. I cannot conceive a *healthy* Spanish culture without his presence. It will, of course, be a different Ortega y Gasset from the one we knew and read: each generation invents its authors. A more European Spain—such as the one currently on the drawing board—will feel greater affinity with the tradition which Ortega y Gasset represents, which is the tradition that has always looked toward Europe. But European culture is living through difficult years and cannot any longer be the fount of inspiration that it was at the outset of this century. Moreover, Spain is also American, as Valle-Inclán admirably saw, while Unamuno, Machado, and Ortega y Gasset himself were blind to it. Nor did the poets of the generation of 1927, though they discovered Neruda, feel or really understand Latin America. Thus the return to Ortega y Gasset will not be a matter of repeating but of amending him.

In this vast, rich, and diverse oeuvre I note three omissions. I have already mentioned two. The first is the look inward, introspection, which is always resolved in irony: he never saw himself and therefore, perhaps, did not know how to smile at his reflection in the mirror. Another is death, the undoing which is all doing. Ortega y Gasset's man is intrepid and his sign is Sagittarius; all the same, though he can look the sun in the face, he never looks at death. The third omission is the stars. In his mental heaven the lively and intelligent stars have vanished, the ideas and essences, the numbers turned light, the ardent spirits which enraptured Plotinus and Porphyry. His philosophy is of thought as action; to think is to do, build, make way, coexist: it is not to see or to contemplate. The work of Ortega y Gasset is a passionate thinking about this world, but from his world many other worlds are lacking, those which constitute the other world: death and nothing, reversals of life, history, and reason; the inner kingdom, that secret territory discovered by the Stoics and explored, before all others, by the Christian mystics; and the contemplation of essences or, as Sister Juana Inés de la Cruz put it, in the only truly philosophical poem in our language, "First Dream," the contemplation of the invisible from here,

> not only of all created things
> under the moon, but of those also
> which, intellectual, lucid, are Stars . . .

Perhaps it could be argued that Ortega y Gasset's thought frees us from worshiping such stars, that is, frees us from the net of metaphysics; ideas are not in any mental heaven: we have invented them with our thoughts. They are not the traces of universal order nor the image of cosmic harmony: they are uncertain lights which guide us on in darkness, signals we make to one another, bridges to cross to the other shore. But this is precisely what I miss in his work: there is no other shore, no other side. The *ratiovitalism* is a solipsism, a cul-de-sac. There is a point at which the Western and Eastern tradition, Plotinus and Nāgār-juna, Chuang-tzu and Schopenhauer, meet: the final end, the supreme good, is contemplation. Ortega y Gasset taught us that to think is to live and that thought separated from living soon ceases to be thought and becomes an idol. He was right, but he cut away the other half of life and thought. Living is also, and above all, to glimpse the other shore, to suspect that there is order, number, and proportion in all that is and that, as Edmund Spenser said, movement itself is an allegory of repose:

> That time when no more Change shall be,
> But stedfast rest of all things firmly stayd
> Upon the pillours of Eternity.
> —"Mutability Cantos"

Because of this, his reflections on history, politics, understanding, ideas, beliefs, love, are a knowledge—not a wisdom.

This essay—written without notes and confiding in my memory—is not an examination of Ortega y Gasset's ideas but of the impression they have left on me. Like so many other Latin Americans of my age, I had passionate recourse to his books during my adolescence and early adulthood. Those readings marked and shaped me. He guided my first steps, and to him I owe some of my first intellectual delights. To read him in those days was almost a physical pleasure, like swimming or walking in a wood. Then I drew back from him. I got to know other countries and I explored other worlds. At the end of the war I settled in Paris. In those days they held in Geneva some international conferences which achieved a certain notoriety. They consisted of a series of six public lectures, given by six European figures and followed, in each case, by discussions in small groups. In 1951 I was invited to participate in these discussions. I accepted: one of the six lecturers was Ortega y Gasset. On the day of his lecture I listened to him emotionally. Also angrily: beside me some provincial French and Swiss professors were making fun of his accent when he spoke in French. On leaving, they wanted to belittle him: I don't know why they were offended. The discussion next day began badly due to the malevolence of these same professors, though, fortunately, a generous and intelligent intervention by Merleau-Ponty put matters straight. I paid little attention to those petty disputes: I wanted to get near Ortega y Gasset and talk to him. At last I managed to do so and the next day I visited him in the Hôtel du Rhône. I saw him there twice. He met me in the bar: a large room with rustic wooden furnishings and a huge window looking out on the impetuous river. A strange sensation: one could see the raging and frothing water falling from a high floodgate, but, because of the thickness of the windowpanes, one could not hear it. I remembered the line from Baudelaire: *Tout pour l'oeil, rien pour les oreilles.*

Despite his love for the German world and its mists, Ortega y Gasset was, in physical and spiritual terms, a man of the Mediterranean. Not wolf nor pine: bull and olive. A vague similarity— stature, manners, coloring, eyes—with Picasso. He could have said with more authority than Rubén Darío: "here, beside the Roman sea / I speak my truth. . . ." I was surprised by the flickering of his bird-of-prey look, I am not sure whether eagle- or hawklike. I realized that, like tinder, he was easily fired, though the blaze did not last long. Enthusiasm and melancholy, according to Aristotle the contradictory extremes of the intellectual temperament. He struck me as proud without being disdainful, which is the best kind of pride. Also open and able to take an interest in his fellow creature. He greeted me openly, invited me to take a seat, and asked the waiter to serve us whiskeys. In answer to his questions, I told him I lived in Paris and that I wrote poems.

149

He shook his head reprovingly and reprehended me: clearly Latin Americans were incorrigible. Then he spoke with grace, openness, and intelligence (why did he never, in his writing, use the familiar tone?) of his age and of his looks (those of a bullfighter who has cut off his pigtail), of Argentinean women (nearer to Juno than to Pallas), of the United States (something might yet sprout there, though it is an excessively horizontal society), of Alfonso Reyes and his little Asiatic eyes (he knew little about Mexico and that seemed to him enough), of the death of Europe and its resurrection, of the bankruptcy of literature, again of age (he said something which would have shaken Plotinus: thinking is an erection and I still think), and of much else.

The conversation tended, at times, toward exposition; then, toward narrative: anecdotes and happenings. Ideas and examples: a master. I sensed that his love of ideas extended to his auditors; he watched me to see if I had understood him. Before him I existed not as an echo; rather, as a confirmation. I understood that all his writings were an extension of the spoken word and that this is the essential difference between the philosopher and the poet. The poem is a verbal object, and though it is made of signs (words), its ultimate reality unfolds beyond those signs: it is the presentation of a form; the discourse of the philosopher uses forms and signs, it is an invitation to realize ourselves (virtue, authenticity, stoic calmness, what have you). I left him with my brain boiling.

I saw him again the next afternoon. Roberto Vernengo, a bright young Argentinean who was his guide in Switzerland and who was well acquainted with German and French philosophy, was with him. We went for a walk in the city. Roberto left us, and Ortega and I walked for a while, returning to his hotel along the bank of the river. Now one could hear the roar of the water falling into the lake. The wind began to blow. He told me that the only activity possible in the modern world was thought ("Literature is dead, it's a store that's closed down, though they still haven't found this out in Paris") and that, to think, one needed to know Greek or, at least, German. He halted for a moment and interrupted his monologue, took me by the arm, and, with an intense look which still moves me, he said: "Learn German and start thinking. Forget the rest." I promised to obey him and accompanied him to the door of his hotel. The next day I took the train back to Paris.

I did not learn German. Nor did I forget "the rest." In this I did follow him, however: he always taught that it is not necessary to think, in itself, that all thought is thought toward or about "the rest." That "rest," whatever name we give it, is our circumstance. "The rest," for me, is history; that which is beyond history is called poetry. We are living an Ending, but ending is no less fascinating and worthy than beginning. Endings and beginnings resemble each other: at the outset, poetry and thought were united; then an act of rational violence divided them; today they tend, almost at random, to come together again. And his third piece of advice: "start thinking"? His books, when I was a young man, made me think. From then on I have tried to be faithful to that first lesson. I'm not too sure that I think now as I did at that time; but I do know that without his thought I could not, today, think at all.

Mexico, October 1980

LUIS BUÑUEL:
THREE PERSPECTIVES

I BUÑUEL THE POET

The release of *L'Age d'or* and *Un chien andalou* signals the first considered irruption of poetry into the art of cinematography. The marriage of the film image to the poetic image, creating a new reality, inevitably appeared scandalous and subversive—as indeed it was. The subversive nature of Buñuel's early films resides in the fact that, hardly touched by the hand of poetry, the insubstantial conventions (social, moral, or artistic) of which our reality is made fall away. And from those ruins rises a new truth, that of man and his desire. Buñuel shows us that a man with his hands tied can, by simply shutting his eyes, make the world jump. Those films are something more than a fierce attack on so-called reality; they are the revelation of another reality which contemporary civilization has humiliated. The man in *L'Age d'or* slumbers in each of us and waits only for a signal to awake: the signal

152

of love. This film is one of the few attempts in modern art to reveal the terrible face of love at liberty.

A little later, Buñuel screened *Land Without Bread*, a documentary which of its genre is also a masterpiece. In this film Buñuel the poet withdraws; he is silent so that reality can speak for itself. If the subject of Buñuel's surrealist films is the struggle of man against a reality which smothers and mutilates him, the subject of *Land Without Bread* is the brutalizing victory of that same reality. Thus this documentary is the necessary complement to his earlier creations. It explains and justifies them. By different routes, Buñuel pursues his bloody battle with reality. Or rather, against it. His realism, like that of the best Spanish tradition— Goya, Quevedo, the picaresque novel, Valle-Inclán, Picasso— consists of a pitiless hand-to-hand combat with reality. Tackling it, he flays it. This is why his art bears no relation at all to the more or less tendentious, sentimental, or aesthetic descriptions of the writing that is commonly called realism. On the contrary, all his work tends to stimulate the release of something secret and precious, terrible and pure, hidden by our reality itself. Making use of dream and poetry or using the medium of film narrative, Buñuel the poet descends to the very depths of man, to his most radical and unexpressed intimacy.

After a silence of many years, Buñuel screens a new film: *Los Olvidados*. If one compares this film with those he made with Salvador Dali, what is surprising above all is the rigor with which Buñuel takes his first intuitions to their extreme limits. On the one hand, *Los Olvidados* represents a moment of artistic maturity; on the other, of greater and more total rage: the gate of dreams seems sealed forever; the only gate remaining open is the gate of blood. Without betraying the great experience of his youth, but conscious of how times have changed, that reality which he denounced in his earlier works has grown even more dense— Buñuel constructs a film in which the action is precise as a mechanism, hallucinatory as a dream, implacable as the silent encroachment of lava flow. The argument of *Los Olvidados*—delinquent childhood—has been extracted from penal archives. Its characters are our contemporaries and are of an age with our own children. But *Los Olvidados* is something more than a realist film. Dream, desire, horror, delirium, chance, the nocturnal part of life, also play their part. And the gravity of the reality it shows us is atrocious in such a way that in the end it appears impossible to us, unbearable. And it is: reality is *unbearable*; and that is why, because he cannot bear it, man kills and dies, loves and creates.

The strictest artistic economy governs *Los Olvidados*. Corresponding to this greater condensation is a more intense explosion. That is why it is a film without "stars"; that is why the "musical background" is so discreet and does not set out to usurp what music owes to the eyes in films; and finally, that is why it disdains local color. Turning its back on the temptation of the impressive Mexican landscape, the scenario is reduced to the sordid and insignificant desolation, but always implacable, of an urban setting. The physical and human space in which the drama unfolds could hardly be more closed: the life and death of some children delivered up to their own fate, between the four walls of abandonment. The city, with all that this word entails of human solidarity, is alien and strange. What we call civilization is for them nothing but a wall, a great No which closes the way. Those children are Mexicans, but they could be from some other country, could live in any suburb of another great city. In a sense they do not live in Mexico, or anywhere: they are the forgotten, the inhabitants of those wastelands which each modern city breeds on its outskirts. A world closed on itself, where all acts are reflexive and each step returns us to our point of departure. No one can get out of there, or out of himself, except by way of the long street of death. Fate, which opens doors in other worlds, here closes them.

In *Los Olvidados* the continuous presence of the hazard has a special meaning, which forbids us from confusing it with mere chance. The hazard which governs the action of the protagonists is presented as a necessity which, nonetheless, *could have been avoided.* (Why not give it its true name, then, as in tragedy: *destiny?*) The old fate is at work again, but deprived of its supernatural attributes: now we face a social and psychological fate. Or, to use the magical word of our time, the new intellectual fetish: an historical fate. It is not enough, however, for society, history, or circumstances to prove hostile to the protagonists; for the catastrophe to come about, it is necessary for those determinants to coincide with human will. Pedro struggles against chance, against his bad luck or his bad shadow, embodied in the Jaibo; when, cornered, he accepts and faces it, he changes fate into destiny. He dies, but he makes his death his own. The collision between human consciousness and external fate constitutes the essence of the tragic act. Buñuel has rediscovered this fundamental ambiguity: without human complicity, destiny is not fulfilled and tragedy is impossible. Fate wears the mask of liberty; chance, that of destiny.

Los Olvidados is not a documentary film. Nor is it a thesis, propagandistic, or moralizing film. Though no sermonizing blurs his admirable objectivity, it would be slanderous to suggest that this is an art film, in which all that counts are artistic values. Far from realism (social, psychological, and edifying) and from aestheticism, Buñuel's film finds its place in the tradition of a passionate and ferocious art, contained and raving, which claims as antecedents Goya and Posada, the graphic artists who have perhaps taken black humor furthest. Cold lava, volcanic ice. Despite the universality of his subject, the absence of local color, and the extreme bareness of his construction, *Los Olvidados* has an emphasis which there is no other word for but *racial* (in the sense in which fighting bulls have *casta*). The misery and abandonment can be met with anywhere in the world, but the bloodied passion with which they are described belongs to great Spanish art. We have already come across that half-witted blind man in the Spanish picaresque tradition. Those women, those drunks, those cretins, those murderers, those innocents, we have come across in Quevedo and Galdós, we have glimpsed them in Cervantes, Velázquez and Murillo have depicted them. Those sticks—the walking sticks of the blind—are the same which tap all down the history of Spanish theater. And the children, the forgotten ones, their mythology, their passive rebellion, their suicidal loyalty, their sweetness which flashes out, their tenderness full of exquisite ferocity, their impudent affirmation of themselves in and for death, their endless search for communion—even through crime—are not and cannot be anything but Mexican. Thus, in the crucial scene in the film—the "libation" scene—the subject of the mother is resolved in the common supper, the sacred feast. Perhaps unintentionally, Buñuel finds in the dream of his protagonists the archetypal images of the Mexican people: Coatlicue [Aztec goddess of death and fertility] and sacrifice. The subject of the mother, a Mexican obsession, is inexorably linked to the theme of fraternity, of friendship unto death. Both constitute the secret foundation of this film. The world of *Los Olvidados* is peopled by orphans, by loners who seek communion and who do not balk at blood to find it. The quest for the "other," for our likeness, is the other side of the search for the mother. Or the acceptance of her definitive absence: the knowledge that we are alone. Pedro, the Jaibo, and his companions thus reveal to us the ultimate nature of man, which perhaps consists in a permanent and constant state of orphandom.

Witness to our age, the moral value of *Los Olvidados* bears no relation at all to propaganda. Art, when it is free, is witness, conscience. Buñuel's work proves what creative talent and artistic conscience can do when nothing but their own liberty constrains or drives them.

Cannes, 4 April 1951

II BUÑUEL'S
PHILOSOPHICAL CINEMA

Some years ago I wrote about Buñuel. This is what I said:

Though all the arts, even the most abstract, have as their ultimate and general end to express and re-create man and his
conflicts, each of them has particular means and techniques of
enchantment and thus constitutes its own domain. Music is
one thing, poetry another, cinema something else again. But
sometimes an artist manages to transcend the limits of his art;
then we engage a work which finds points of reference outside
its world. Some of the films of Luis Buñuel—*L'Age d'or, Los
Olvidados*—while they remain films, take us toward other
boundaries of the spirit: some of Goya's engravings, a poem
by Quevedo or Péret, a passage from Sade, an absurd character
from Valle-Inclán, a page of Gómez de la Serna. . . . These films
can be enjoyed and judged as film and at the same time as
something which belongs to the wider and freer world of those
works, precious among all others, which have as their object
not only to reveal human reality to us but also to show us a
way to transcend it. Despite the obstacles which the real world
sets in the way of similar projects, Buñuel's attempt develops
under the double arch of beauty and rebellion.

In *Nazarin*, with a style that flees from all complacency and
rejects all suspect lyricism, Buñuel tells us the story of a quixotic
priest, whose concept of Christianity soon sets him at odds
with the Church, society, and the police. Nazarin belongs, like
many of Galdós's characters, to the great tradition of Spanish
madmen. Their madness consists of taking Christianity seriously and of trying to live in accordance with the Gospels. The
man who refuses to admit to himself that what we call reality
is reality and not just an atrocious caricature of the true reality,
is mad. Like Don Quixote, who discerned his Dulcinea in a
peasant girl, Nazarin perceives in the monstrous sketches of

157

Andra the whore and Ujo the hunchback the helpless image of fallen men; and in the erotic delirium of Beatriz, an hysteric, he perceives the disfigured face of divine love. In the course of the film—in which scenes in the best and most terrible Buñuel manner, now with more concentrated and therefore more explosive rage, abound—we witness the *cure* of the madman: that is, his torture. Everyone rejects him: the powerful and self-satisfied because they consider him a nuisance and, in the end, dangerous; the victims and the persecuted because they need another, more effective type of consolation. He is pursued not only by the powers that be, but by social equivoque. If he begs for alms, he is an unproductive person; if he seeks work, he breaks the solidarity of the salaried. Even the sentiments of the women who pursue him, reembodiments of Mary Magdalen, turn out ambiguous in the end. In the jail where his good works have landed him, he receives the final revelation: his "goodness," quite as much as the "evil" of one of his companions in punishment, a murderer and church-robber, are equally useless in a world which worships efficiency as the highest value.

Faithful to the tradition of the Spanish madman, from Cervantes to Galdós, Buñuel's film tells the story of a disillusionment. For Don Quixote, illusion was the chivalric spirit; for Nazarin it is Christianity. But there is something more. As the image of Christ fades in Nazarin's consciousness, another begins to emerge: that of man. Buñuel makes us witness, by means of a series of episodes that are exemplary in the good sense of the word, a double process: the disappearance of the illusion of divinity and the discovery of the reality of man. The supernatural gives place to the marvelous: to human nature and its powers. This revelation is embodied in two unforgettable moments: when Nazarin offers *otherworldly consolations* to the dying lover and she replies, gripped by the image of her beloved, with a phrase that is genuinely frightening: *no to heaven, yes to Juan*; and at the end, when Nazarin rejects the alms of a

poor woman, only to accept them after a moment of doubt—
no longer as a gift but as a token of comradeship. Nazarin
the loner has ceased to be alone: he has lost God but he has
found men.

This little text appeared in a handout that accompanied the
showing of *Nazarin* at the Cannes Film Festival. It was feared,
rightly as it proved, that confusion would arise over the meaning
of the film, since it is not only a criticism of social reality but
also of the Christian religion. The risk of confusion, which all
works of art run, was greater in this instance because of the nature
of the novel which inspired Buñuel. Galdós's theme is the old
opposition between the Christianity of the Gospel and its eccle-
siastical and historical distortions. The hero of the book is a
rebellious and enlightened priest, a true Protestant: he abandons
the Church but stays with God. Buñuel's film sets out to show
the opposite: the disappearance of the figure of Christ from the
consciousness of a sincere and pure believer. In the scene of the
dying girl, which is a transposition of Sade's "Dialogue Between
a Priest and a Dying Man," the woman affirms the precious,
irrecoverable value of earthly love: if there is a heaven, it is here
and now, in the moment of the carnal embrace, not in a timeless,
bodiless beyond. In the prison scene, the sacrilegious bandit appears no less absurd a man than the enlightened priest. The crimes
of the former are as illusory as the holiness of the latter: if there
is no God, there is no sacrilege or holiness either.

Nazarin is not Buñuel's best film, but it is typical of the duality
that governs his work. On the one hand, ferocity and lyricism,
a world of dream and of blood which immediately calls to mind
two other great Spaniards: Quevedo and Goya. On the other,
the concentration of a style not at all baroque in character which
leads him to a kind of exasperated sobriety. The straight line,
not the surrealist arabesque. Rational rigor: each of his films,
from *L'Age d'or* to *Viridiana*, is unfolded as a *demonstration*.

The most violent and free imagination at the service of a syllogism honed sharp as a knife, irrefutable as a rock: Buñuel's logic is the implacable reason of the Marquis de Sade. This name clarifies the relationship between Buñuel and surrealism: without that movement he would have been a poet and a rebel anyway; thanks to it, he sharpened his weapons. Surrealism, which revealed Sade's thought to him, was not for Buñuel a school of rapture but of reason: his poetry, while it remained poetry, became criticism. In the closed cloister of criticism, rapture spread its wings and clawed its own breast with its nails. Bullring surrealism, but also critical surrealism: the bullfight as philosophical demonstration.

In a primary text of modern letters, *De la Litterature Considerée comme une Tauromachine* (*Of Literature Considered as an Art of Bullfighting*), Michel Leiris points out that his fascination with bullfighting depends on the fusion between risk and style: the *diestro* (skilled matador)—the Spanish word is exact—should face the bull's charge without losing composure. True: good manners are indispensable for dying and for killing, at least if you believe, as I do, that these two biological acts are at the same time rites, ceremonies. In bullfighting, danger achieves the dignity of form, and form the veracity of death. The bullfighter locks himself into a form which opens out on the danger of dying. It is what in Spanish we call *temple* (temper): musical intrepidity and fine tuning, hardness and flexibility. The bullfight, like photography, is an exposure, and the style of Buñuel, by matched artistic and philosophical choice, is that of exposure. To expose is to expose oneself, risk oneself. It is also to externalize, to show and to demonstrate: to reveal. Buñuel's stories are an exposure: they reveal human realities as they submit them, as if they were photographic plates, to the light of criticism. Buñuel's bullfight is a philosophical discourse, and his films are the modern equivalent to Sade's philosophical novel. But Sade was an original philosopher and a middling artist: he did not realize that art, which loves rhythm and litany, excludes repetition and reiteration. Buñuel is an artist, and his films are subject not to poetic but philosophical reproach.

The reasoning which governs all Sade's work can be reduced to this idea: man is his instincts, and the true name of what we call God is fear and mutilated desire. Our morality is a codification of aggression and humiliation; reason itself is nothing but an instinct which knows itself to be instinct and which is afraid of being so. Sade did not set himself the task of proving that God does not exist: he took this for granted. He wanted to demonstrate what human relations would be like in an effectively atheist society. This is the essence of his originality and the unique character of his attempt. The archetype of a republic of truly free men is the Society of the Friends of Crime; of the true philosopher, the ascetic libertine who has managed to achieve impassiveness and who ignores laughter and tears alike. Sade's logic is total and circular: he destroys God but he does not respect man. His system can give rise to many criticisms, but not to that of incoherence. His negation is universal: if he affirms anything it is the right to destroy and be destroyed. Buñuel's criticism has a limit: man. All our crimes are the crimes of a phantom: God. Buñuel's theme is not man's guilt, but God's. This idea, present in all his films, is more explicit and direct in *L'Age d'or* and in *Viridiana*, which are for me, with *Los Olvidados*, his fullest and most perfect creations. If Buñuel's work is a criticism of the illusion of God, that distorting glass which will not let us see man as he is, what are men *really* like and what sense will the words love and fraternity have in a *really* atheist society?

Sade's answer does not satisfy Buñuel, of course. Nor do I believe that, at this time of day, he rests content with the descriptions which offer us philosophical or political utopias. Apart from the fact that these prophecies cannot be verified, at any event not yet, it is clear that they do not correspond to what we know about man, his history and his nature. To believe in an atheist society governed by natural harmony—a dream we have all had—would be today like repeating Pascal's wager, only in the opposite sense. More than a paradox, it would be an act of despair: it would command our admiration, not our assent. I do not know what answer Buñuel could give to these questions. Surrealism, which denied so many things, was motivated by a gale of generosity and faith. Among its ancestors are counted not only Sade and Lautréamont but also Fourier and Rousseau. And perhaps it is the last of these, at least for André Breton, who is the true origin of the movement: exaltation of passion, unlimited confidence in the natural powers of man. I do not know if Buñuel is closer to Sade or to Rousseau; it is more likely that both conduct an argument within him. Whatever his beliefs on this score, it is the case that in his films neither Sade's nor Rousseau's answer appears. Reticence, timidity, or disdain, his silence is troubling. It is troubling not only because it is the silence of one of the great artists of our time, but also because it is the silence of all the art of this first half-century. After Sade, as far as I know, no one has dared to discover an atheist society. Something is lacking in the work of our contemporaries: not God, but man without God.

Delhi, 1965

III CANNES, 1951:
LOS OLVIDADOS

I must have been about seventeen when I first heard of Luis Buñuel. I was a student at the National Preparatory School and I had just discovered, in the display cases of the Porrua and Robredo bookstores, near San Ildefonso, the books and magazines of the new literature. In one of these publications—*La gaceta literaria* (*The Literary Gazette*), which Ernesto Jiménez Caballero published in Madrid—I read an article on Buñuel and Dali. This article was illustrated by both of them, with reproductions of Dali's paintings and stills from their two films: *Un chien andalou* and *L'Age d'or*. The stills excited me more deeply than the pictures by the Catalan painter: in the film images, the mixture of everyday reality and madness was more effective and explosive than in the mannerist illusionism of Dali. A few years later, in the summer of 1937 in Paris, I met Buñuel face to face.

One morning, at the door of the Spanish consulate, where I had gone with Pablo Neruda to pick up a visa, we bumped into him. Pablo stopped him and introduced us. It was a fleeting encounter. That same year I managed at last to see the two famous films, with the smell of cordite in the air: *Un chien andalou* and *L'Age d'or*. For me, the second film was, in the strict sense of the word, a revelation: the sudden appearance of a truth hidden and buried, but alive. I discovered that the age of gold is in each of us and that it has the face of passion.

Many years later, in 1951, again in Paris, I saw Luis Buñuel again at the house of some friends: Gaston and Betty Bouthoul. During that period I saw him quite often; he came to my house, and finally one day he called to entrust me with a mission: I was to present his film *Los Olvidados* at that year's Cannes Festival. I accepted enthusiastically, without hesitation. I had seen the film at a private showing with André Breton and other friends. A strange detail: the night of the showing, at the other end of the little projection room, Aragon, Sadoul, and others were present. When I saw them I thought for a moment that a pitched battle would ensue, as in the days of their youth. I exchanged glances with Elisa Breton, who showed signs of nervousness; but all and sundry sat down silently and a few minutes later the showing began. I think it was the first time Aragon and Breton had seen each other since their rift, twenty years before. The film moved me: it was animated by the same violent imagination and for the same implacable reason as *L'Age d'or*, but Buñuel, through using a very strict form, had managed a greater concentration. As we left, Breton praised the film, though he regretted that the director had conceded too much, at certain points, to the realist logic of the story at the expense of the poetry or, as he said, of the marvelous. For my part, I thought that *Los Olvidados* showed the way not to overcome superrealism—can anything be overcome in art and literature?—but to unravel it; I mean that Buñuel had found an exit from the superrealist aesthetic by inserting, in the traditional form of the narrative, the irrational images which spring up out of the dark side of man. (In those years I set myself a similar task in the more restricted domain of lyric poetry.) And here perhaps it is not out of place to say that in the best works of Buñuel a rare faculty is revealed, a faculty which could be called *synthetic imagination*, that is, totality and concentration.

As soon as I got to Cannes I met with the other Mexican delegate. He was a producer and exhibitor of Polish origin who lived in Paris. He said he was aware of my nomination as Mexican delegate to the festival and he pointed out that our country had sent another film to the festival. In fact, Buñuel was participating in the festival in his own right, invited by the French organizers. The Mexican delegate also told me that he had seen *Los Olvidados* in Paris, and it seemed to him, despite its artistic merits, an esoteric film, aestheticist and at times incomprehensible. In his judgment, it had no chance whatsoever of winning any prize. He added that various Mexican high functionaries, as well as numerous intellectuals and journalists, were against the showing at Cannes of a film that denigrated Mexico. This last point was unfortunately true, and Buñuel has referred to the subject in his memoirs (*My Last Sigh*), though discreetly, without naming his critics. I will follow his example, but not without stressing that, in this attitude of theirs, the two evils which at that time our progressive intellectuals suffered from came together: nationalism and socialist realism.

The skepticism of my colleague in the Mexican delegation was made up for by the enthusiasm and goodwill that various friends, all admirers of Buñuel, showed, among them the legendary Langlois, director of the Cinématheque de Paris, and two young superrealists, Kyrou and Benayoun, who put out an avant-garde magazine, *L'Age du cinéma*. We visited many notable artists who lived in the Côte d'Azur, inviting them to the event at which the film was to be shown. Almost all of them accepted. One of those most keen to show himself in favor of Buñuel and of free art was, to my surprise, the painter Chagall. On the other hand, Picasso proved evasive and reticent; in the end, he didn't show up. I recalled his hardly friendly attitude to Apollinaire in the matter of the Phoenician statuettes. Most generous of all was the poet Jacques Prévert. He lived in Vence, a few kilometers from Cannes. Langlois and I went to see him, we told him our worries, and a few days later he sent us a poem in praise of Buñuel which we hurried into print. I believe it caused a certain stir among the critics and journalists attending the festival.

I wrote a little essay as a kind of introduction. Since we had no money we mimeographed it. On the day of the showing I handed it out to all comers at the door of the theater. A few days later a Paris newspaper printed it. Buñuel's film immediately occasioned many articles, commentaries, and discussions. *Le Monde* praised it to the skies, but *L'Humanité* called it "a negative film." Those were the years of socialist realism, and the *positive message* was exalted as the central value of works of art. I remember the furious argument I had one night shortly after the showing with Georges Sadoul. He told me Buñuel had *deserted* the true realism and that he was paddling, though talentedly, in the sewage of bourgeois pessimism. I replied that his use of the word *desert* revealed that his idea of art was worthy of a sergeant and that with the theory of socialist realism the intention was to conceal the null Soviet social reality. . . . The rest is known: *Los Olvidados* did not get the grand prix, but with that film begins Buñuel's second and great creative period.

Mexico, 1983

165

JORGE GUILLÉN

Jorge Guillén is a Spaniard from Castile, which doesn't mean he's more Spanish than the Spaniards of other regions but that he is Spanish in a different way. He is no purist: Guillén is a European Spaniard and belongs to an historical moment in which Spanish culture was opening out to the thought and art of Europe. But unlike Ortega, who enlivened and inspired that group, Guillén was closer to France than to Germany. He pursued his university studies in Paris, where he was married first and where he taught. He also gave courses at Oxford. He returned to Spain and promptly became a leading figure of a generation which Gerardo Diego introduced in 1925 in a celebrated anthology. It was a generation parallel to the one that in Mexico gathered around the magazine *Contemporáneos*. The Civil War scattered the Spanish poets. Guillén lived for years in the United States.

For much of his life he has been a university professor. He has lived for long stretches in Italy, where he married for the second time. A whole European. Also a complete Spanish-American: he knows our continent and has friends in all our countries.

His work is extensive and almost entirely in verse. Three books: *Cántico* (*Canticle*), *Clamor* (*Tumult*), and *Homenaje* (*Homage*). The subtitles are illuminating: *Cántico: Fe de vida* (*Faith in Life*)— affirmation of being and affirmation of what is. This book has had very great influence on our language. *Clamor: Tiempo de historia* (*The Time of History*)—the poet in the corridors—errors and horrors—of contemporary history. *Homenaje: Reunión de vidas* (*Joining of Lives*)—the poet not among men or confronting them but with them. And above all with women: Guillén is a poet for whom woman exists. I am sure he would agree if he heard me say that woman is the highest form of being. *Reunión de vidas*, with poets living as well as dead: in that book Guillén converses with his masters, his antecedents in the poetic art, and his contemporaries and successors. When he began writing he was thought a severe poet; now we realize that he has also been an extremely fecund poet: in 1973 he published a new book, simply called *Y otros poemas* (*And Other Poems*).

Guillén belongs to a group of writers who knew they were part of a tradition that transcends linguistic frontiers. All of them felt that they were not only German, French, Italian, or Spanish but European. The European consciousness, a victim of nationalisms, is progressively attenuated until it almost vanishes in the nineteenth century. Its rebirth, at the beginnings of this century, is something Europe had not experienced since the eighteenth century. Examples of this sensibility include Rilke, Valéry Larbaud, Ungaretti, Eliot. Here I should mention two Latin Americans: Alfonso Reyes and Jorge Luis Borges. It is instructive to note that all of them wrote in their native language and in French—except Borges, who has written in English. In those years Paris was still the center, if not of the world, at least of art and literature. . . . In that Paris of the first third of the century Guillén spent decisive formative years. The Paris of Huidobro had been one of revolt in art and poetry: Picasso, Reverdy, Tzara, Arp, the beginnings of surrealism. Guillén is nearer to the *Nouvelle Revue Française* and, above all, to *Commerce*, the great poetry magazine edited by Paul Valéry, Leon Paul Fargue, and Valéry Larbaud—the great Larbaud, friend of Gómez de la Serna, Reyes, Güiraldes.

Because of his classical bent Guillén suggests a Mediterranean Eliot. But literary essays and critical writing do not occupy the same place in Guillén's work as they do in Eliot's. And there is something else which radically distinguishes him from Eliot: in his work there is scarcely a trace of Christianity. His subject is sensual and intellectual: the world touched by the senses and the mind. Profoundly Mediterranean poetry, Guillén is very near to Valéry. He was his friend, experienced his influence, and his translation of "Le cimetière marine" is a masterpiece. All the same, the similarities between Valéry and Guillén do not cancel out the deep differences. Valéry is a spirit of prodigious insight, one of the truly luminous minds of this century. He is a great writer endowed with two qualities which in others appear opposed: intellectual rigor and sensuality. But these admirable and unique gifts are as if lost in a kind of vacancy: unsupported, they lack world. The I, the consciousness, has swallowed the world. This evaporation of reality, is it the price the skeptic must pay if he wants to make sense to himself? I doubt it. Hume was no less a skeptic, and yet his work has an architecture which Valéry's lacks. Valéry's powers of deconstruction were greater than his powers of construction. His *Cahiers* are an imposing ruin. Valéry was a most powerful spiritual lever which lacked a pivot point. Guillén's critical and analytical powers are not as great as Valéry's, but his spiritual lever did not lack a pivot.

For Guillén reality is what we touch and see: faith in the senses is the poet's true faith. This provides him common ground with certain painters. Not the realists but rather an artist like Juan Gris, in whom the rigor of abstraction is fused with a fidelity to the physical object. In Guillén, good Mediterranean that he is, sensuality is dominant, and this draws him toward another great painter, Matisse. These names, it seems to me, trace Guillén's spiritual profile: his lucidity calls Valéry to mind; his almost ascetic rigor before the object allies him with Juan Gris; the line which swerves like a feminine river evokes Matisse. But the light which illuminates his poetry is that of the Castilian plains, the light which shines down to us from Fray Luis Ponce de León and his Horatian odes.

Guillén returned to Spain in 1924. He was thirty years old. He had not yet published a book. He was a late developer, unlike Lorca and Alberti. The panorama of Spanish poetry in those days was extremely rich. Never since the seventeenth century had Spain had so many excellent poets. That was the best period of Juan Ramón Jiménez. It was also the period of his influence on the young writers. Juan Ramón was writing a simple, inspired poetry in the traditional vein of the Spanish lyric: songs, romances, *coplas*, and other popular forms. Short poems, almost exclamations; fresh poems, sudden fountains. Poetry of popular rhythms and yet aristocratic, refined, and as is clear to us today, a boneless poetry, without architecture, excessively subjective. Though the young poets followed Juan Ramón, their images came from creationism and ultraism. Huidobro's system of metaphor had stirred the poets of Latin America and Spain a few years earlier. A strong but very Spanish amalgam of traditionalism and avant-garde: Alberti composed madrigals to the train ticket and Salinas songs to the radiator.

There was much talk in those years of "pure poetry." Juan Ramón defined it as the simple, the plain and refined: a word reduced to the essential. In fact, Juan Ramón was not defining "pure poetry" so much as his own poetry. Guillén was returning from France, where the notion of "pure poetry" was also in the ascendant. The French conception was more rigorous. Abbé Bremond had defined "pure poetry" with a nondefinition: it was the undefinable, what is beyond sound and sense, something which was confused with prayer and ecstasy. Though for Valéry poetry was neither gibberish nor prayer, his definitions too were, in their apparent simplicity, enigmatic: poetry was all that which could not be said in prose. But what can't be said in prose? In a letter to a friend Guillén defines his position in brief. It is typical of Guillén to formulate his poetic in a letter to a friend: Huidobro had launched various manifestos, and others of us have written essays and even books. It is worth quoting part of his letter, well known though it is:

> Bremond has been and remains useful. He represents the popular apologetic, like a poet-catechist for Sunday morning. And his lecture is a sermon. But how far all this mysticism is, with its metaphysical and ineffable phantom, from pure poetry, according to Poe, to Valéry and the young poets of there and here! Bremond speaks of poetry in the poet, of a *poetic state*, and that's already a bad sign. No, no. There is no poetry but that achieved in the poem and there is no way to set against the poem an *ineffable state* which is corrupted when it is carried out.... Pure poetry is mathematics and chemistry—nothing more—in the good sense of that expression suggested by Valéry and which some young mathematicians and chemists have made their own, understanding it in a different sense, but always within that initial, fundamental direction. Valéry himself repeated it to me, once, one morning in the rue de Villejust. Pure poetry is all that remains in the poem after all that is not poetry has been eliminated. *Pure* is the same as *simple* in chemical terms. . . . Since I call *pure, simple*, I come down resolutely on the side of composed, complex poetry, the poem with poetry and other human things. In sum, quite a pure poetry, *ma non*

troppo, if one takes as the unit of comparison the *simple* element in its greatest inhuman and superhuman theoretical rigor.

Guillén denied that there were "poetic states": poetry is in the poem, is a verbal deed. This attitude radically separated him not only from Bremond but, at the other extreme, from the surrealists, who attributed more importance to the poetic experience than to the act of writing poems. Guillén was aware that, whatever else, a purely poetic poetry would be quite boring. And something more serious: it was linguistically impossible since language is by nature impure. A "pure poetry" would be one in which language had ceased to be language. The idea of "pure poetry" was very much of its period. Years before, physics had tried to isolate the ultimate components of matter. For their part, the cubist painters reduced objects to a series of relations on a plane. Following the example of the physicists and painters, as Jakobson has more than once recalled, the linguists had attempted to discover the ultimate elements of language, the signifying particles. This intellectual orientation was powerfully manifest in the work of Edmund Husserl, the phenomenologist. The philosophers of this persuasion, too, attempted to reduce things to their essences, and thus regional ontologies of the chair, the pencil, the claw, the hand were made. Unfortunately, these ontologies almost always ended in expressions such as these: The chair is the chair, poetry is poetry (or: all that is not prose). Phenomenology issues, I'm afraid, in tautologies. But tautology is, perhaps, the only metaphysical affirmation which men can reach. The most we can say about being is that it is.

MOST CRITICS HAVE INSISTED on the ontological character of "Mas alla," the opening poem of *Cantico*: affirming what is and affirming being. I have always looked a little distrustfully at philosophical explanations of poetry. Still, in this instance, interpretation can serve us as a point of departure for a fuller understanding of the poem, so long as we do not forget even for a moment that "Mas alla" is not a philosophical treatise but a poem. The ideas of the poem interest and arouse us not because they are true but because Guillén has made them poetically true. The axis on which "Mas alla" turns, and more generally, the axis of all the poetry in *Cántico*, is an affirmation which appears at the beginning and end of the poem: *quiero ser* (I want to be). Two-edged phrase: I want being and I want to be. This double and universal wanting is already present in Plato: all beings want to be because the supreme good is being. That is why Saint Augustine thought that evil was nothing but the absence of being.

Generally speaking, also since Plato, being is identified with essence. What is the being of the chair, table, star? Its essence, its idea. Ultimate realities, essential realities, are ideas: intellectual forms we can contemplate, whether in the starry sky or in the space, at once ideal and subject to the senses, of the geometric bodies. But Guillén's poem does not affirm being as essence or as idea but as passing: being is blood and time, eternity suspended. An eternity which is manifest in dates, places, and circumstances: today, Monday, in this room, in the morning. Is this a form of materialism? No, the ultimate reality is neither material nor ideal: it is a wanting, a relationship, an interchange. We have before us a paradoxical realism since it supports itself by affirming the instant as eternity.

Guillén's realism looks like relativism. It is established on flux, that is, on time. When the poem begins, huge time surrounds the sleeper. Later, made energy, it manifests itself in things. That energy moves things and changes them. The world is relation because it is time which is movement which is passing which is change. Movement of one thing toward another and change of one thing into another. Here Guillén's universalizing strategy comes into play: being—an absolute—becomes relative, becomes particular and is manifest in this and that; this and that are relative, are time, are instants, but each instant is all time, each instant is a totality. The now becomes forever, a forever that is happening now and is happening for ever. Here is wherever, and wherever is the center of the universe. First movement: being is not an essence or an idea: it is a passing, an energy crystallized in a here and now. Second movement: here is central, the point toward which all points converge; and the now is an always which is an instant, a suspended eternity. Man is the agent of this transmutation. Or rather: man's desire to be is. The desire is his and his alone: at the same time, it is the desire of all creatures and all things. It is a universal wanting. What is more, the plural universe is a desire to be in unison.

Man is the point of intersection of this plural universe of desire, and that is why each man is central. But man is central not because he is the creation of the demiurge. Man is not king of creation nor the favorite son of the creator. Man is the point of intersection between chance and necessity. I use deliberately the title of the book by the biologist Jacques Monod—*Chance and Necessity*—because there is a curious coincidence between Guillén's poetic thought and contemporary biology. For Guillén, man's being is at the same time the expression of universal totality—his body follows its circuit well, as those of the stars do—and the result of a chance collision of forces and energies: atoms, cells, acids. Another biologist, François Jacob, says that cells have no function but to reproduce, copy, and duplicate themselves. We might say that they are in love with themselves, like Narcissus and like Luzbel. Sometimes, when they copy themselves, by a well-understood principle of physics, changes occur. These are mutants. These mutants pass through the strainer of natural selection; some vanish, and others, as they grow strong, perpetuate themselves until they give rise to new species. But the cells of Jacob and Monod are a desire to be which only wants to be, while Guillén's will to be is, like that of all men, a desire to be which contemplates itself, reflects itself, and, above all, speaks. It is an accord which does not recognize itself as such. Man rescues the instant when he speaks it, names it. The present endures not only and exclusively because, like the cells, it repeats itself, but because it sees itself through the moment. In that momentary apparition, consciousness accedes to a kind of vertiginous eternity—and names it. An eternity which lasts as long as it takes the poet to say it and us to hear it. It is enough.

Man—that universal desire of being and that desire of universal being—is a moment of change, one of the forms in which energy is manifest. That moment and that form are transitory, circumstantial: here and now. That moment will disappear, that form will be scattered. Nonetheless, that moment includes all moments, is all moments; that form binds itself with all forms and is in every part. How do we know this? We know it without knowing it. We feel it when we live certain experiences. For example, when we wake up. Except that really to wake up we must take account of the fact that the world in which we wake up is a world which wakes up with us. Without eyes and soul man could not know that each minute is on the crest of time and at the center of space. But eyes and soul are not enough: the world is incomprehensible, the ultimate reality is invisible, untouchable. No matter: we have language. By means of the words we get close to things, we call them *evidences, prodigies, riddles, transcendencies*. Language is a dike against nameless chaos. The world of relations which is the universe is a verbal world: we wander among things which are names. We ourselves are names. Landscapes of names which time unceasingly destroys. Wasted names which we have to invent anew each century, each generation, every morning when we wake up. Poetry is the process by which man names the world and names himself. That is why man is the legend of reality. And I would add, the legend of himself.

Guillén's here and now resemble the instant which dissolves

all instants. It is the instant of lovers and also that of mystics, especially Eastern ones, with which Guillén is perhaps not acquainted, and whom he would probably disapprove of if he knew them. That instant annuls the contradiction between this and that, past and future, negation and affirmation. It is not the union, the marriage of contraries, but their scattering. On this vision of the other aspect of being—the blank aspect: vacancy—it is not easy to erect a metaphysic. But it is possible to build a wisdom and above all a poetics. It is an experience which we have all lived and which some have thought. Poets are those who, whatever their beliefs, language, and age, manage to express it.

In *Mediciones*, 1979

Two Notes on José Revueltas: Christianity and Revolution

When the armed struggle ceased and what has come to be called "the constructive phase of the Mexican Revolution" began, two different forms of artistic expression, the novel and painting, avidly addressed themselves to the recent past. The consequences of this engagement have been the "Mexican school of painting" and the "Novel of the Revolution." Over the last twenty years the novel has served to express the authors' nostalgias, hopes, and disillusions with the revolution, rather than any more literary undertakings. Technically poor, these works are more picturesque than descriptive, more in the nature of genre writing than realism. . . . The novelists of the revolution, and among them the great myopic talent of Mariano Azuela, blinded by the frenzy of gunpowder or by that other frenzy of the corrupt generals' diamonds, have reduced their theme to that: many deaths, many crimes and lies. And a superficial stage set of burned villages, maddening jungles, and godless deserts. In this way they have mutilated fictional reality—the only reality that matters to the true novelist—by reducing it to a pure chronicle or a framed portrayal of customs. All the "Novels of the Revolution" have been narratives and chronicles, even those of Mariano Azuela. (Valéry Larbaud declared that Martín Luis Guzmán reminded him of Tacitus: a strange way to praise a novelist!)

The next generation has hardly attempted the novel. Made up as it is by a group of literati, poets, and essayists, it has shown a degree of repugnance, if not disdain, for the realities which surround it. The novel has been the Cinderella of these writers, who rally under the banner of curiosity and evasion. After them, there have been isolated attempts: those of the most recent group of Mexican writers (Juan de la Cabada, Efrén Hernández, Rubén Salazar Mallén, Andrés Henestrosa, Rafael Solana, Francisco Tario). Almost all of them evince a marked preference for that hard and strict genre, the short story. Just as in painting the generation of "muralists" has been succeeded by a group of young artists which a patronizing North American critic dubbed the "little masters," so these new Mexican prose writers, successors to the "Novelists of the Revolution," have excelled above all in the writing of short stories and narratives. One of Juan de la Cabada's books, *Paséo de mentiras* (*Passage of Lies*), brings together in a few pages some stories and a novella which make him, up to now, the most interesting and enigmatic of all; one novel, *Camino de perfección* (*Road of Perfection*), and particularly some bitter and harsh stories, lead one to believe that Rubén Salazar Mallén also has the necessary talent to give Mexico a real novel.

The most ambitious and impassioned—and the youngest, too—is José Revueltas (twenty-seven years old, affiliated from the age of fourteen with the Communist Party; his political ideas have given him a chance to get to know the insides of the country's jails several times, in the time of President Rodríguez). José Revueltas has published a first novel, *El luto humano* (*Human Sorrow*), which has received an award in a national competition. Before that he had written some mysterious, stammering stories; a short novel, *El quebranto*,* and a narrative, *Los muros de agua* (*The Walls of Water*), in which he tells of the life of a penal colony in the Pacific. (He was imprisoned there for two years, before he reached the age of twenty.) Revueltas's novel has aroused both the most ardent praise and the sourest criticism. A Marxist critic has charged him with pessimism, but other enthusiasts have been quick to cite Dostoevski.

El luto humano tells a dramatic story: a group of peasants goes on strike at an "irrigation system" established by the Mexican Revolutionary government. The strike and the consequent drought cause the government plan to fail and the exodus begins. Only three families insist on staying on in that deserted place. One day the river, dry until that time, swells and breaks its banks and a flood isolates the characters of the novel on a rooftop. Alcohol, hunger, and jealousy finish them off. The novel opens when the river begins to swell and ends just as the buzzards settle down to devour the dying. All these events take place in a period of a few days. But the novel scarcely alludes to what the peasants actually do to escape the flood; Revueltas prefers to tell us what they think, what they remember, what they feel. Often he displaces his characters; in their place he expounds his own doubts, his faith and his despair, his opinions about death or about Mexican religiosity. The action is interrupted each time a character, before dying, summarizes his life. . . . A constant religious concern invades the work: Mexicans, pious by nature, and lovers of blood, have been deprived of their religion, without the Catholic faith having been enough to satisfy their hard thirst for eternity.

---

*It was never published in full, except for the first chapter (*Taller* 2, April 1939), because Revueltas lost the manuscript.

Adam, a murderer, who believes himself to be the embodiment of Fate, and Natividad, a murdered leader, symbolize, in very religious terms, the past and future of Mexico. Between them move the rancorous present-day Mexicans, and their taciturn women represent the earth, thirsty for water and blood, a baptism that combines, together with agricultural fertility rites, ancient Aztec and Christian rites. In the closing pages the author tries to convince himself—more than the reader—that by a better use of natural resources and a better distribution of wealth, this religiosity without hope, this blind love of death, will vanish from the Mexican soul. The novel is clearly contaminated with sociology, religion, and ancient and modern Mexican history. There is some contamination in the language, which is at times brilliant, at times strangely turgid.

These faults damn the work, but not its author. Because, oddly, the reader feels himself infected with the same fascination to which the novelist is prey. Revueltas feels a kind of religious revulsion, of love composed of horror and repulsion, for Mexico. True, Revueltas has not written a novel, but, all the same, he has cast light into himself. Seduced as much by the myths of Mexico as by its realities, he has made himself a part of that drama which he attempts to depict. Endowed with talent, imaginative force, quite uncommon vigor and sensibility—and devoured by a haste which does not let him, it would seem, linger over his faults— José Revueltas is now ready to write a novel. In this attempt he frees himself of all his phantoms, all his doubts and opinions. As is the case with much Mexican painting, which reveals a great vigor that often remains outside the picture, beyond the frame, Revueltas has brought together all his great modeling and prophetic power, but without managing to apply it to his object: the novel. In short, for what am I reproaching Revueltas? I reproach him—I now realize—for his youth, since all those defects, that lack of soberness in the language, that desire to say it all at once, that lack of concentration and that reluctance to trim the useless wings of words, ideas, and situations, that absence of discipline—within and without—these are nothing but the faults of youth. In any event, Revueltas is the first writer among us who has tried to create a deep work, remote from genre writing, superficiality, and the cut-price psychology which dominate today. Perhaps nothing will remain of this work of his but its spirit: isn't this enough for a young man who is just starting, and starting us, on the task of creating for ourselves an imaginative world, strange and disturbingly personal?

Sur, July 1943

SECOND NOTE

When I reread the preceding note, which Luis Mario Schneider dug out of an old issue of *Sur*, I immediately felt the need to clarify, correct, and extend it. It is one beginner's criticism of another beginner; what is more, it is far too cutting and categorical. My excuse is that those faults are frequent among the young. I end by reproaching Revueltas for his youth, and that censure is perfectly applicable to the opinion I held at that time. Youth does not justify other errors. For instance, in the first paragraph I condemn the novelists of the Mexican Revolution. That was a silliness: among them there are two excellent writers, Martín Luis Guzmán and Mariano Azuela. Both were masters of their art. Martín Luis Guzmán's prose, bright as that of a Roman historian, has a kind of classical transparence: its subject is terrible, but he traces it with a calm, firm rhythm. Azuela was not "a great myopic talent"; nor was he dull: he was a lucid writer, in control of his resources, and he explored many roads which others have traveled since. But when I wrote my note on *El luto humano* (1943), the novel of the revolution had turned itself from a movement into a school: the invention was now a recipe. In this sense I was not wrong: the appearance of *El luto humano*, published a few years before *Al filo del agua* by Augustín Yañez (1947), was a break and a beginning. Despite its imperfections, Revueltas's novel set something in motion which is not yet exhausted.

My analysis of *El luto humano* is too brisk. I point out with excessive severity the narrator's unskillful devices and the frequency with which his voice displaces that of his characters. Those defects are due, at least in part, to the difficulty and novelty of what Revueltas was setting out to say and what he managed to say more felicitously years later. The young novelist wanted to use the new techniques of the North American novel (the Faulkner of *The Wild Palms* is constantly present) to write a chronicle that was at once epic and symbolic, about an episode which seemed to him to possess the quality of a revolutionary exemplum. The purpose was contradictory: Faulkner's realism (perhaps all realism) implies a pessimistic view of man and of his earthly destiny; in its turn, Revueltas's epic chronicle is undermined by religious symbolism, for lack of a better expression. The peasants fight for land and water, but the novelist continually suggests that that fight alludes to another, one not entirely of this world. Though my note stresses the religiosity of Revueltas, it does not describe its paradoxical character: a vision of Christianity *within* his Marxist atheism. Revueltas lived his Marxism as a Christian, and that is why he lived it, in Unamuno's sense, as agony, doubt, and negation.

In speaking of the religiosity of the Mexican people, I mention "rancor," an inexact word. I attribute it to the great catastrophe of the Conquest, which deprived the Indians not only of their world but of their otherworld: that of their gods and mythologies. Still, when with the key of baptism it unlocked the gates of heaven and hell for them, Catholicism paradoxically gave them the possibility of coming to terms with their old religion. Perhaps Revueltas thought that, "on a higher historical plain," revolutionary Marxism would perform in the face of Christianity the same

181

function that Christianity performed in the face of the pre-Columbian religions. This idea would explain the importance of the Christian symbolism in the novel. Moreover, he was always fascinated by popular beliefs and myths. A friend told me how once, half in jest, half seriously, it occurred to Revueltas to celebrate a marriage rite not before the altar of the Virgin of Guadalupe but before the goddess Coatlicue in the Museum of Anthropology. I remember too that on the night of the 1971 Corpus Christi massacre, when a number of friends were gathered at Carlos Fuentes's house and we discussed what we might do, Revueltas approached me and with an undefinable smile on his face whispered in my ear: "Let's all go dance before the Holy Lord of Chalma!" A phrase reveals a man: "Atheism," André Breton once told me, "is an act of faith." The *witticisms* of Revueltas were oblique confessions.

At the end of my note I point to the real significance of *El luto humano*: "Revueltas has not written a novel, but . . . he has cast light into himself." Today I would say: that work was a stage in his pilgrimage, a real Way of the Cross, toward the light. And this is the source of the central question, which Revueltas faced bravely from his very short novel, *El quebranto*, and which he never stopped asking himself: What light, the light *here*, or *there*? Perhaps here is there, perhaps revolutions are nothing but the road that here travels toward there. Revueltas's action seems to be secretly inspired by this idea. He was a militant revolutionary, novelist, and author of philosophical and political essays. As a militant he was a dissident who criticized with identical passion capitalism and bureaucratic "socialism"; the same duality is evident in his novels, stories, and essays. Thus, on the one hand, there is a remarkable continuity between his life and his work: it is impossible to separate the novelist from the militant and the militant from the author of texts of philosophical, aesthetic, and political criticism; on the other hand, that unity contains a fracture, an excision. Revueltas was in a continual dialogue—or more precisely, a permanent dispute—with his philosophical, aesthetic, and political ideas. His criticism of Communist orthodoxy was self-criticism at the same time. His case is not unique, of course; on the contrary, it is more and more common: the dissidence of Marxist intellectuals is one expression, perhaps the central one, of the universal crisis of that doctrine. But there is something that sets Revueltas's doubts and criticisms apart from the others: the tone, the religious passion. And there is something more: the questions which Revueltas time and again asked himself make no sense and cannot be answered except within a religious frame of reference. Not that of just any religion but specifically that of Christianity.

For Westerners the opposition between atheism and religion cannot be resolved. This has not been the case with other civilizations: in its strictest and purest form, Buddhism is atheist. And yet that atheism does not root out the divine: like all beings, without excepting men or the Buddha himself, the gods are bubbles, reflections of emptiness. Buddhism is a radical critique of reality and the human condition: the true reality, *sunyata*, is an undefinable state in which being and nonbeing, the real and the unreal, cease to be at odds and, in coming together, annul themselves. Thus history is nothing but shadow play, illusion—like everything else. This is also why Buddhist religious observance is essentially contemplative. By contrast, for Christianity the incarnation of Jesus and his sacrifice are deeds that are at once supernatural and historical. Not only does divine revelation unfold in history, but history is the testing ground for Christians: souls triumph and are lost here, in this world. The Marxist Revueltas takes on the Christian heritage with all its consequences: the weight of human history. The nexus between Christianity and Marxism is history; both are doctrines which identify with the historical process. The condition in which Marxism is possible is the same as that for Christianity: action on this world. And the rivalry between Marxism and Christianity is manifest here on earth: to fulfill himself and his mission, revolutionary man has to evict God from history. The first revolutionary act is the critique of Heaven. The relation between Marxism and Christianity implies, at the same time, a bond and a breach. Buddhism— in general terms, all Eastern thought—ignores or disdains history. At the same time, immersed in an atmosphere of the divine, surrounded by gods, it does not acknowledge the notion of a unique creator God. Oriental atheism is not really atheistic; in a strict sense, only Jews, Christians, and Moslems can be atheists: they are believers in a single creator God. Bloch very rightly said: "Only a true Christian can be a good atheist; only a true atheist can be a good Christian."

The Christian Marxism of Revueltas can only be understood from the double perspective I have just sketched. In the first place, the idea of history conceived as a process endowed with meaning and direction; secondly, irreducible atheism. Now, between history and atheism a further opposition opens out: if God disappears, history ceases to mean. Christian atheism is tragic because, as Nietzsche saw it, it is a negation of meaning. For Dostoevski, if there is no God, everything is permissible, everything is possible; but if everything is possible, nothing is: the infinity of possibilities annuls them and resolves them in impossibility. In the same way: the absence of God makes everything thinkable; but everything equals nothing: everything and nothing are not thinkable. Atheism sets us face to face with the unthinkable and the impossible; that is why it is terrifying and, literally, unbearable. Also, that is why we have installed other deities in God's vacant niche: Reason, Progress. These principles come down to earth, become incarnate and turn into the secret activators of history. They are our Christs: the nation, the proletariat, the race. In Revueltas's novel, the old man is called Adam, like our father; and the new man, the collective Christ, is called Nativity. The history of the Son of Man begins with the Nativity and culminates with the Sacrifice; the Revolution obeys the same logic. That logic is rational, "scientific": historical materialism; and it is supernatural: transcendence. The "scientific" is explicit; the supernatural, implicit. Divine transcendence disappears, but, surreptitiously, by means of revolutionary action it continues to function. As Bloch also said, revolution is "to transcend without transcendence."

The hostility between Marxism and Christianity never entirely disappears but it is attenuated if the terms change places. For Christianity we men are sons of Adam, the child of God. In the beginning is God, who is not only the giver of meaning but the creator of life. God is before history and after it: he is the beginning and the end. For a Christian Marxist like Bloch or Revueltas, God cannot be before; in fact, God does not exist: the original, primordial reality is man or, better said, human society. But historical man is hardly man at all; to realize himself, truly to be man, he must pass through the trials of history, must triumph over it and transform its fatal course into liberty. Revolution makes men of men—and more than men: man's future is to be God. Christianity was the humanizing of God; revolution promises divinity to man. Abrupt change of places: God is not before but after, not the creator of men but their creature. Bloch alters the Biblical phrase and says *I am what I will be* (Ernst Bloch, *L'athéisme dans le christianisme*, Gallimard, 1978).

Revueltas never formulated his ideas with Bloch's clarity, but the *temper* of his writings and his life corresponds to this agonizing and contradictory vision of Marxism and Christianity. Of course, he reached these attitudes independently and by his own route. It was not philosophy that guided him but his personal experience. In the first place, the religion of his childhood; then his interest in Mexican common life, all of it impregnated with religiosity; and finally, his philosophical and poetic temperament. This last was decisive: Revueltas asked himself philosophical questions which Marxism—as among others Kolakowski and Bloch himself have recognized—cannot answer except with scientistic commonplaces. In fact, those questions have only metaphysical and religious answers. Metaphysics, after Hume and Kant, is forbidden to us moderns. Thus Revueltas resorts intuitively and with passion, in a movement back to the earliest elements in his being, to the religious answers, mingled with the millenarian ideas and hopes of the revolutionary movement. Though philosophy enthralled him, he was above all a creative artist. His religious temperament drew him to communism, which he saw as the way of sacrifice and communion; that same temperament, inseparable from the love of truth and the good, led him at the end of his life to a criticism of bureaucratic "socialism" and Marxist clericalism.

Marxism has turned into an ideology and today functions as a pseudoreligion. The transformation of a philosophy into an ideology and of this into a religion is not a new phenomenon: the same thing happened with Neoplatonism and Gnosticism. Nor is the transformation of a religion into a political power and of a priesthood into a clerical bureaucracy anything new: Roman Catholicism has known these perversions. The historical peculiarity of communism is in the fact that it is not really a religion but an ideology that works as though it were a science, the Science; thus, it is not a church but a party which does not resemble other parties so much as the militant orders and brotherhoods of the Catholics and Moslems. Communist parties begin as little sects but as soon as they grow, they turn into closed churches. (I use the plural because in the Communist movement schisms and divisions proliferate.) Each church believes that it possesses universal truth; this pretension would not be perilous were it not for the fact that the bureaucracies which govern these groups are motivated by an equally universal desire to dominate and proselytize. Each member of each church is a missionary and each missionary a potential inquisitor. Revueltas's religiousness was far removed from these ideological fanaticisms; his true spiritual affinities are to be found on the other side, near the primitive Christians, the fourth-century Gnostics, and the Protestant rebels and revolutionaries of the Reformation. Within the Catholic Church he would have been as much a heretic as he was within the Communist orthodoxy. His Marxism was not a system but a passion, not a faith but a doubting and, to use Bloch's terminology, a hope.

It was no less difficult for Revueltas to live with himself than it was for him to live with his Communist comrades. For years he tried to be a disciplined militant, and each attempt ended in a breach and expulsion. He used the Hegelian dialectic to postpone the definitive breach; like so many others, he told himself that evil is a snare of history so that it might the better fulfill itself, that denial is a moment in the process which inevitably turns into affirmation, that the revolutionary tyrants are tyrants in order to protect liberty, and that—as the Spanish theologians of the seventeenth century and in the twentieth century Prosecutor Vishinsky and the Bolsheviks tried in 1936 and 1938 have brilliantly proven—the guilty are innocent and the innocent guilty. These are the riddles of divine will or of historical necessity. The justification of evil began with Plato; in his retractions and recantations, Revueltas did nothing more than pursue a two-thousand-year-old tradition. As the Neoplatonist Proclus said, matter itself "is good, despite being infinite, obscure and formless." (For the ancients infinity was an imperfection since it lacked form.) But the resources of dialectics are exhausted while the evil expands without ceasing. In the end Revueltas had to confront the reality of bolshevism and his own reality. He did not resolve this conflict—who has ever managed to do that?—but he had the courage to formulate it and think it through. He loyally lived out his inner contradiction: his atheist Christianity, his agonized Marxism. Many praise the courage with which he suffered prisons and hardships on account of his ideas. It's true, but it must be borne in mind, too, that Revueltas practiced another kind of heroism, no less difficult and austere: intellectual heroism.

His work is uneven. Some pages seem to be rough drafts rather than definitive texts; others are remarkable and entitle him to a unique and separate place in Mexican literature: *Los dias terrenales*, *Los errores*, *El apando*, and, above all, the stories of *Dios en la tierra* and *Dormir en tierra*, many of them admirable. But the literary excellence of these works, considerable though it is, does not altogether explain his attractiveness. In our world everything is relative, good and evil, pleasure and pain. Though the majority are content, a few rebel and, possessed by a god or by a devil, demand *everything*. They thirst and hunger for the absolute. Don't ask me to define it: the absolute is by definition undefinable. Revueltas suffered from that hunger and that thirst; to satisfy them he was writer and he was revolutionary. If I look among modern Mexicans for a kindred spirit, I have to go to the opposite ideological camp and to an earlier generation: to José Vasconcelos. Like Revueltas, he had a passionate nature but was unable to subject his passion to discipline; he was a writer of impulses and prophecies, copious and careless, sometimes dull and other times luminous. For both, political action and metaphysical adventure, historical polemic and meditation, were interconnected. They united the active life with the contemplative or, more accurately, the speculative life: in their works there is not really disinterested contemplation—what I take to be the highest wisdom—but meditation, reflection, and, in his best moments, spiritual flight. The work of Vasconcelos is larger and richer than that of Revueltas, but no deeper or more intense. But the point is, they belong to the same psychic family. They are the opposite of Reyes, who made an absolute of harmony; and of Gorostiza, who adored perfection with so exclusive a love that he preferred to be silent rather than write something less than perfect.

Despite their spiritual resemblance, Vasconcelos and Revueltas took very different roads. Nourished on Plotinus and believing in his mission as a crowned philosopher, Vasconcelos felt he had been sent down from on high: that is why he was an educator;

Revueltas believed in the rebel apostles and saw himself as an emissary of the lower world: that is why he was a revolutionary. The spiritualist Vasconcelos never doubted: the devil—that spirit of denial and patron of philosophers—did not tempt him: the world tempted him (power) and the flesh (women). Vasconcelos confessed that he had desired his neighbor's wife and that he had fornicated with her, but he never admitted that he had made a mistake. The only sins which the materialist Revueltas confessed to were sins of the spirit: doubts, denials, errors, pious lies. In the end he repented and undertook the criticism of his ideas and of the dogmas in which he had believed. Vasconcelos did not repent; he exalted Christian humility the better to cover his foes with invectives; Revueltas, in the name of Marxist philosophy, undertook an examination of his conscience which Saint Augustine and Pascal would have appreciated and which impresses me on two counts: for the scrupulous honesty with which he performed it and for the subtlety and depth of his analysis. Vasconcelos ended up in the embrace of Catholic clericalism; Revueltas broke with the Marxist clerisy. Which of the two was the true Christian?

Mexico D.F., 12 April 1979

LUIS CERNUDA:
THE EDIFYING WORD

I

In 1961 the *Mercure de France* devoted an issue to Pierre Reverdy, who had recently died. Luis Cernuda wrote a few pages valuable not so much for what they say about Reverdy as for what they reveal, obliquely, about Cernuda himself: how he identifies poetic conscience with ethical purity, his taste for the essential word, which, not always justly, he set against what he called the sumptuousness of the Spanish and French traditions. But I recall that article not to stress the affinities between the French and the Spanish poet—though the influence of Reverdy on Cernuda would be worth pursuing—but because what Cernuda wrote three years ago on the destiny of dead poets seems today to have been thought and said about his own death: "What country suffers its poets with pleasure? Its living poets, I mean, since there is no country which doesn't adore its dead poets." Spain is no exception. Nothing is more natural than that the literary journals of the Iberian peninsula should publish homages to the poet: "Since Cernuda has died, long live Cernuda"; nothing is more natural, again, than that poets and critics, all together, cover with the same gray sediment of praises the oeuvre of a spirit which with admirable and inflexible obstinacy never stopped affirming his dissidence. When the poet is buried, we can discourse without risk about his work and make it say what it seems to us it ought to have said: where he wrote separation, we will read union: God where he said devil; homeland, not inhospitable land; soul, not body. And if "interpretation" is impossible, we will erase the forbidden words: rage, pleasure, nausea, boy, nightmare, solitude. . . . I do not want to suggest that all those who praise him try to whitewash what was black, nor that they do this entirely in bad faith. It's not a deliberate lie but a pious substitution. Perhaps without being aware, moved by a sincere desire to justify their admiration for a work which their conscience reproves, they transform a particular and unique truth—sometimes unbearable and repellent, like all that is truly fascinating—into a general and inoffensive truth, acceptable to all. Much of what has been written recently on Cernuda could have been written about any other poet. There have even been those who affirm that death has returned him to his native land ("When the dog is dead, rabies are at an end"). One critic, who claims he knows Cernuda's work well and admires it, does not hesitate to write: "The poet had a tragic fault: the inability to recognize any other kind of love but romantic love; thus conjugal love, paternal and filial love, were all closed doors for Cernuda." Another critic is of the view that the poet "has found a world in which reality and desire are in harmony." Has that writer asked himself what that paradise would be like, and what its angels and divinities would be?

Cernuda's work is an exploration of himself; a proud affirmation, in the last account not without the humility of its irreducible difference. He said it himself: "I have only tried, like every man, to find my truth, my own, which will not be better or worse than that of others, only different." To serve his memory, it is useless to build him monuments which, like all monuments, conceal the dead, but rather it is necessary to go deeply into that different truth and set it against our own. Only then will his truth, because it is distinct and irreconcilable, come near to our own truth, which is neither better nor worse than his, but our own. The work of Cernuda is a road toward our own selves. That is what gives it its moral value. Because, despite being an excellent poet—or, more accurately, *because* he was one—Cernuda is one of the very few moralists Spain has given us, in the sense in which Nietzsche is the great moralist of modern Europe and, as he said, "its first psychologist." The poetry of Cernuda is a criticism of our values and beliefs; in it destruction and creation are inseparable, since what it affirms implies the dissolution of what society regards as just, sacred, or immutable. Like Pessoa's, his work is a subversion, and his spiritual fecundity resides in the fact that he puts to the test the systems of collective morality, both those established on the authority of tradition and those which social reformers propose to us. His hostility to Christianity is no less intense than the repugnance he feels for political utopias. I am not suggesting that one has to agree with him; but I do say that, if we really love his poetry, we must *hear* what he is actually saying. He does not seek a pious reconciliation with us; he expects of us that most difficult thing: recognition.

II

In the following notes I have no intention of running through the entire body of Cernuda's work. I write without having to hand his most important books, and, beyond what an acquaintance of many years' standing with his work has left on my memory, I do not possess more than a handful of his poems in an anthology, the third edition of *Ocnos* and *Desolación de la quimera*. I once wrote that his development was like the growth of a tree, in contrast to the verbal constructs of other poets. That image was only partly just: trees grow spontaneously and fatedly, but they lack consciousness. A poet is one who is conscious of that fatedness, I mean one who writes because he cannot help it—and knows it. He is an accomplice of his fate—and its judge. In Cernuda, spontaneity and reflection are inseparable, and each stage of his work is a new attempt at expression and a meditation on what he expresses. He never ceases advancing into himself, and at the same time asking himself if he is really advancing. Thus, *La realidad y el deseo* can be seen as a spiritual biography, a succession of lived moments, and a reflection on those vital experiences. Thence his moral character.

Can a biography be poetic? Only if the anecdotes are transmuted into poems, that is, only if the deeds and the dates cease to be history and become exemplary. But exemplary not in the didactic sense of the term but in the sense of "notable action," as when we say: unique example. Or: myth, ideal argument and real fable. The poets help themselves to legends in order to tell us real things; and with real events they create fables, examples. The dangers of poetic biography are twofold: the unsolicited confession and the unasked counsel. Cernuda does not always avoid these extremes and it is not unusual for him to stray into confidences and moralism. No matter: the best of his work lives in that real or imaginary space of myth. A space as ambiguous as the very figure it sustains. Real fable and ideal history, *La realidad y el deseo* is the myth of the modern poet. Though a descendant, a being different from the *poet maudit*. The doors of hell have shut, and for the poet not even the resource of Aden or Ethiopia is left: wandering the five continents, he always lives in the same room, talks to the same people, and his exile is everybody's. Cernuda did not know this—he was too intent upon himself, too abstracted in his uniqueness—but his work is one of the most impressive personal testimonies to this truly unique situation of modern man: we are condemned to a promiscuous solitude and our prison is as large as the planet itself. There is no exit or entrance. We move from the same to the same. Seville, Madrid, Toulouse, Glasgow, London, New York, Mexico City, San Francisco: was Cernuda really in those cities? Where are those places in fact? All the ages of man appear in *La realidad y el deseo*. All, except infancy, which is evoked only as a lost world whose secret has been forgotten. (What poet will give us, not the vision or the nostalgia of childhood, but childhood itself, who will have the courage and the genius to talk as children do?) Cernuda's book of poems could be divided into four parts: adolescence, the years of apprenticeship, in which he surprises us with his exquisite mastery; youth, the great moment when he discovers passion and discovers himself, a period to which we owe his most beautiful blasphemies and his best love poems—love of love; maturity, which begins as a contemplation of earthly powers and ends in a meditation on human works; and the final period, already at the last boundary of old age, his gaze more precise and reflexive, his voice more real and bitter. Different moments of a single word. In each period there are admirable poems, but I prefer the poetry of his youth ("Los placeres prohibidos," "Un rio un amor," "Donde habite el olvido," "Invocaciones") not because the poet is entirely in possession of himself in them but precisely because he is not: a moment in which guessing has yet to become certitude, certitude formula. His early poems seem to me to be an exercise whose perfection does not exclude affectation, a certain man-neredness from which he never entirely freed himself. His mature books evince a plaster classicism, that is, a neoclassicism: there are too many gods and gardens; there is a tendency to confuse eloquence with diction, and it is indeed odd that Cernuda, con-stant critic of that inclination of ours toward the "noble tone," did not perceive it in himself. Finally, in his last poems reflection, explication, and even impertinences take up too much space and displace song; the language does not have the fluidity of speech but the written dryness of discourse. And yet, in all those periods there are poems which have enlightened and guided me, poems to which I always return and which always reveal something essential to me. The secret of that fascination is twofold. We are in the presence of a man who invests himself entirely in every word he writes and whose voice is inseparable from his life and his death; at the same time, that word never renders itself to us directly: between us and it is the poet's face, the reflection which creates distance and thus permits the true communication. Conscience gives depth, spiritual resonance, to what it says; the thinking unfolds a mental space which gives the word seriousness. Conscience gives unity to this vast and varied oeuvre. Fated poet, he is doomed to speak and to consider what he says. For this reason, at least in my reading, his best poems are those from the years in which spontaneous diction and thought fuse; or those of the moments of maturity in which passion, rage, or love give him back his old enthusiasm, only now in a language that is harder and more lucid.

La realidad y el deseo, biography of a modern Spanish poet, is also the biography of a European poetic conscience. Because Cernuda is a European poet, in the sense in which Lorca or Machado, Neruda or Borges, are *not* European. (The Europeanism of Borges is very American: it is one of the modes we Latin Americans have of being ourselves or, rather, of inventing ourselves. Our Europeanism is not an eradication or a turning to the past: it is an attempt to create a temporal space before a timeless space and thus to embody it.) Of course the Spanish are Europeans, but the genius of Spain is polemical: it fights with itself, and each time it attacks one part of itself, it attacks a part of Europe. Perhaps the only Spanish poet who feels himself a natural European is Jorge Guillén; for this reason, also naturally, he feels himself firmly planted in Spain. By contrast, Cernuda chose the European with the same fury with which others of his contemporaries decided to be natives of Andalusia, Madrid, or

Catalonia. His Europeanism is polemical and is tinged with anti-Spanish sentiment. Revulsion for the native land is not exclusive to the Spanish, it is a constant in modern European and American poetry. (I think of Pound and of Michaux, of Joyce and of Breton, of cummings . . . the list would be endless.) Thus Cernuda is antagonistic to Spain for two reasons: because of his polemical Spanishness and because of his modernity. As to the first, he belongs to the family of the Spanish heterodox; as to the second, his work is a slow reconquering of the European heritage, a search for that central current from which Spain set itself apart a long time ago. It is not a matter of influences—though like any poet he has suffered many, most of them beneficial—but of an exploration of himself, not now in a psychological sense but of his history.

Cernuda discovers the modern spirit by way of surrealism. He has often said how seductive Reverdy's poetry was for his sensibility—Reverdy, master of the surrealists and his own. In Reverdy he admires the "poetic asceticism"—equivalent, he claims, to Braque's—which makes him build a poem with the minimum of verbal material; but more than the economy of his means he admires his *reticence*. That word is one of the keys to Cernuda's style. Seldom have bolder thought and more violent passion made use of more chaste expressions. Reverdy was not the only Frenchman to overwhelm him. In a letter dated 1929 written from Madrid, he asks a friend in Seville to return various books to him (*Les pas perdus* of André Breton, *Le libertinage* and *Le paysan de Paris* of Louis Aragon) and adds: "Azorín, Valle-Inclán, Baroja: what does all that stupid, inhumane, rotten Spanish literature matter to me?" Let purists not be too scandalized. In those same years Breton and Aragon found that French literature was equally inhumane and stupid. We have lost that lovely unbuttonedness; how much harder it is now to be insolent, unjustly just, than in the 1920s.

What does Cernuda owe to the surrealists? The bridge between the French avant-garde and Spanish-language poetry was, of course, Vicente Huidobro. After the Chilean poet, contacts increased and Cernuda was neither the first nor the only one to have felt the fascination of surrealism. It would not be difficult to point out in his poetry and even in his prose the traces of certain surrealists, such as Eluard, Crevel, and, though he is a writer at the opposite pole from him, the dazzling Louis Aragon (in his early manner). But unlike Neruda, Lorca, or Villaurrutia, for Cernuda surrealism was something more than a lesson in style, more than a poetic or a school of verbal and imagistic associations: it was an attempt to embody poetry in life, a subversion which embraced language quite as much as institutions. A morality and a passion. Cernuda was the first and almost the only one who understood and made his own the true meaning of surrealism as a movement of liberation—not of verse but of consciousness: the last great spiritual shaking-out of the West. To the psychic commotion of surrealism must be added the revelation of André Gide. Thanks to the French moralist, Cernuda accepts himself; from that time on his homosexuality was not to be a sickness or a sin but a destiny freely accepted and lived. If Gide reconciles Cernuda with himself, surrealism will serve him to set his psychic and vital rebellion within a vaster, more total subversion. The "forbidden pleasures" open a bridge between this world of "codes and rats" and the underground world of dream and inspiration: they are earthly life in all its taciturn splendor ("marble members," "iron flowers," "earthly planets") and they are also the highest spiritual life ("exalted solitude," "memorable freedoms"). The fruit these harsh liberties offer us is one of mystery, whose "taste no bitterness corrupts." Poetry turns active; the dream and the word cast down the "anonymous statues"; in the great "hour of vengeance, its brilliance can destroy your world." Later Cernuda abandoned surrealist mannerisms and tics, but his essential vision, though his aesthetic was different, remained that of his youth.

Surrealism is a tradition. With that critical instinct which distinguishes great poets, Cernuda traces the current back: Mallarmé, Baudelaire, Nerval. Though he kept faith with these poets, he did not stop at them. He went to the source, to the origin of modern Western poetry: to German romanticism. One of his themes is that of the poet confronting a world hostile or indifferent to men. Present in his earliest poems, from "Invocaciones" on, it develops with an increasingly somber intensity. The figure of Hölderlin and those of his descendants are his model; soon those images are transformed into another, entrancing and terrible: that of the devil. Not a Christian devil, repulsive and terrifying, but a pagan one, almost a boy. It is his double. Its presence is to be a constant in his work, though it changes with the years and each time its words sound more bitter and hopeless. In the image of the double, always the untouchable reflection, Cernuda seeks himself but he also seeks the world: he wants to know that he exists and that others exist. The others: a race of men different from men.

Beside the devil, the companionship of dead poets. Reading Hölderlin and Jean Paul and Novalis, Blake and Coleridge, is something more than discovery: a recognition. Cernuda goes back to his own. Those great names are living persons, invisible but dependable intercessors. He talks with them as if he talked with himself. They are his true family and his secret gods. His work is written thinking of them: they are something more than a model, an example, or an inspiration: they are a gaze that judges him. He has to be worthy of them. And the only way to be worthy is to affirm his truth, to be himself. The moral theme reappears. But it will not be Gide, with his psychological morality, but Goethe who will guide him in this new phase. He does not seek a justification but an equilibrium; what the young Nietzsche called "health," the lost secret of Greek paganism: the heroic pessimism which created tragedy and comedy. Often he spoke of Greece, of its poets and philosophers, of its myths, and, above all, of its vision of beauty: something which is neither physical nor corporeal and which is perhaps only a musical chord, a measure. In *Ocnos*, when he speaks of "beautiful knowledge"—because he knows beauty or because all knowledge is beauty?—he says that beauty is measure. And thus, by a road which leads from surrealist rebellion to German and English romanticism and from there to the great Western myths, Luis Cernuda recovers his double heritage as a poet and as a Spaniard: the European tradition, the sense and savor of the Mediterranean noon. What began as a polemical and unbounded passion ends in a recognition of measure. A measure, it is true, in which other things—also of the West—do not fit. Among them, two of the greatest: Christianity and woman. "Otherness" in its most absolute manifestations: the other world and the other half of this one. Nonetheless, Cernuda makes a virtue of necessity and creates a universe in which two essential elements are not lacking, one peculiar to Christianity, the other to woman: introspection and the mystery of love.

I have not spoken of another influence which was of the first importance both on his poetry and on his criticism, especially after *Las nubes* (1940): modern English poetry. In his youth he loved Keats and later on felt himself drawn toward Blake, but these names, especially the latter, belong to what could be called his demonic or subversive half: they nourished his moral rebelliousness. His interest in Wordsworth, Browning, Yeats, and Eliot is different in kind: he seeks in them not so much a metaphysic as an aesthetic conscience. The mystery of literary creation and the theme of the ultimate significance of poetry—its relations with truth, with history, and with society—always concern him. In the reflections of the English poets he found—formulated in a way different from or similar to his own—answers to these questions. One evidence of this interest is the book he devoted to the poetic thought of the English lyric poets. I believe I am right in thinking that T. S. Eliot was the living writer who exerted the most profound influence on the mature Cernuda. I repeat: an aesthetic, not a moral or metaphysical influence: the reading of Eliot did not have the liberating effects that his discovery of Gide had done. The English poet makes him see the poetic tradition with new eyes, and many of his studies of Spanish poets are composed with that precision and objectivity, not without eccentricity, which are among the charms and perils of Eliot's critical style. But the example of this poet can be seen not only in Cernuda's critical opinions but also in his creative work. His encounter with Eliot coincides with the change in his aesthetic; having assimilated the experience of surrealism, he does not bother to seek new forms but rather to express himself. Not a norm but a measure, something which neither the French moderns nor the German romantics could give him. Eliot had felt a similar necessity, and after *The Waste Land* his poetry is poured out into increasingly traditional molds. I could not say whether this attitude of return, in Cernuda and in Eliot, benefited or harmed their poetry; in one sense, it impoverished them, since surprise and invention, the wings of the poetry, disappear to some extent from their mature work; in another sense, perhaps without that change they would have become mute or impoverished in a sterile search, as happens with great creators such as Pound and cummings. And it is commonplace that nothing is more tedious than the professional innovator. In a word, Eliot's poetry and criticism helped Cernuda to moderate the romantic he always was.

Cernuda had a predilection, from the first, for the long poem. For modern taste poetry is, above all, verbal concentration, and therefore the long poem faces an almost insuperable problem: to bring together extension and concentration, development and intensity, unity and variety, without making the work a collection of fragments and without recourse to the vulgar expedient of amplification, either. *Un coup de des*, maximum verbal concentration in a little over two hundred lines, some of them a single word in length, is an example, to my mind the highest example, of what I want to say. It is not the short poem but the long one that requires the use of scissors; the poet should exercise remorselessly his gift of elimination if he wants to write something that isn't prolix, dispersed, or diffuse. Reticence, the art of saying the unsaid, is the secret of the brief poem; in the long poem silences do not work suggestively, do not speak, but are like the divisions and subdivisions of musical space. More than a form of writing, they are a form of architecture. Mallarmé had already compared *Un coup de des* to a partita, and Eliot had called one of his great compositions *Four Quartets*. Cernuda thought it was the best poem Eliot had written, and we often discussed his reasons for this preference, since I was drawn to *The Waste Land*—which, of course, ought also to be regarded as a musical construction.

Though our poet did not learn the art of the long poem from Eliot—he had written them before reading Eliot, and some of them are among the most perfect poems he made—the English writer's ideas clarified his own and partly modified his conceptions. But ideas are one thing, the temperaments of each another. It would be useless to seek in his work the principles of *harmony*, *counterpoint*, or *polyphony* which inspire Eliot and St.-John Perse; and nothing could be more remote from the "simultaneity" of Pound or Apollinaire than the linear development, like that of vocal music, of Cernuda's poems. The melody is lyrical, and Cernuda is only, and outstandingly, a lyric poet. Thus the form most congenial to his nature was the monologue. He wrote monologues throughout his life, and it could even be said that his work is a long monologue. English poetry showed him how monody can turn back on itself, unfold and question itself: it taught him that monologue is always dialogue. In one of his studies, he alludes to the lesson of Robert Browning; I would add that of Pound, who was the first to exploit the monologue of Browning. (Compare, for instance, the use of questions in "Near Périgord" and in the long late poems of Cernuda.) And here I think I ought to say something on a subject which troubled him and about which he wrote pages of great insight: the relations between spoken language and the poem.

Cernuda points out that the first writer to proclaim the poet's right to employ "the language really used by men" was Wordsworth. Though it isn't altogether correct to say that this precedent is the origin of the so-called prosaicism of contemporary poetry, it is as well to distinguish between this idea of Wordsworth's and Herder's, who saw in poetry "the song of the people." Popular language, if indeed it exists and is not just an invention of German romanticism, is a survival from feudal times. It is a form of nostalgia to cultivate it. Jiménez and Antonio Machado always confused "popular language" with spoken language, and that is why they identify the latter with traditional song. Jiménez thought that "popular art" was simply the traditional imitation of aristocratic art; Machado believed that the true aristocracy resided in the people and that folklore was the most refined art. However different these points of view appear to us, both reveal a nostalgic view of the past. The language of our time is different: it is the language spoken in the great city, and all modern poetry, from Baudelaire on, has made that language the point of departure for a new lyricism. As a reaction against the aesthetic of the exquisite and singular which the Latin American poets had made fashionable, the simplicity of the so-called popular Spanish poetry is no less artificial than the complications of the symbolists. Influenced by Jiménez, the poets of Cernuda's generation made of ballad and of song their favorite genre. Cernuda never succumbed to the affectation of the popular (an affectation to which we owe, all the same, some of the most seductive poems of our modern lyricism) and tried to write as one speaks; or rather: he set himself as the raw material of poetic transmutation not the language of books but of conversation. He did not always succeed. Often his verse is prosaic, in the sense in which *written* prose is prosaic, not living speech: something more considered and constructed than said. Because of the words he uses, almost all of them correct, and because of an overfastidious syntax, Cernuda sometimes "talks like a book" rather than "writes as one speaks." What is miraculous is that that writing should suddenly condense into scintillating expressions.

In Campoamor Cernuda perceived an antecedent of poetic prosaicism; if he had been, it would be a regrettable antecedent. One shouldn't confuse philosophical table-talk with poetry. The truth is that the only modern Spanish poet who has used *naturally* the spoken language is the forgotten José Moreno Villa. (The only one and the first one, *Jacinta la pelirroja*, was published in 1929.) In fact, the first to use the poetic possibilities of prosaic language were, strange as it may seem, the Latin American modernists: Darío and, most of all, Leopoldo Lugones. In Campoamor's poems, the end-of-century rhetoric decays into expressions which are pseudophilosophical commonplaces and thus constitutes an example of what Breton calls the "descending image." The symbolists set the colloquial idiom face to face with the artistic to produce a clash within the poem, as one can see in *Augurios* by Rubén Darío, or else they make the urban speech the raw material of the poem. This latter procedure is that of the Lugones of the *Lunario sentimental*. Toward 1915, the Mexican poet López Velarde learned the lesson of the Argentinean poet and managed to fuse the literary and spoken language together. It would be tedious to mention all the Latin American poets who, after López Velarde, make prosaicism a poetic language; six names will suffice: Borges, Vallejo, Pellicer, Novo, Lezama Lima, Sabines. . . . Strangest of all, this comes not from English poetry but from the master of Eliot and Pound: the symbolist Jules Laforgue. The author of the *Complaintes*, not Wordsworth, is the source of this trend, both among the English and among the Latin Americans.

Often it is said of Cernuda, and more generally of the poets of his generation, that they "close" a period of Spanish poetry.

I confess that I do not know what this means. For something to "close"—if it is not a definitive ending—it is necessary for something or someone to open another period. The Spanish poets themselves, beyond odious comparison, do not seem to me to have initiated a movement; I would even say that, as far as the matter of language and vision is concerned—and that is what counts in poetry—they come over as singularly timid. This is not a reproach: the second romantic generation was no less important than the first and it gave us a central name: that of Baudelaire. Novelty is not the sole poetic criterion. In Spain there has been a change of tone, not a break with the past. That change is natural, but it shouldn't be confused with a new era. Cernuda neither closes nor opens an era. His poetry, unmistakable and distinct, forms part of a universal tendency which in the Spanish language begins, a little behind time, at the end of the last century and which is still not over. Within that historical period his generation, in Latin America and in Spain, occupies a central place. And one of the poets central to that generation is—Luis Cernuda. He did not create a common language or style, as Rubén Darío and Juan Ramón Jiménez did in their day or, more recently, Vicente Huidobro, Pablo Neruda, and Federico García Lorca. Perhaps on this rests his value and his future influence: Cernuda as a poet is a loner for loners.

In a tradition which has used and abused but seldom reflected on words, Cernuda represents the conscience of the language. A similar example is that of Jorge Guillén, except that while for him poetry lives—to use the jargon of the philosophers—at the realm of being, Cernuda's is temporal: human existence is his domain. In both poets, more than *reflection*, we find poetic meditation. Reflection is an extreme and total process: the word turns upon itself and denies itself a meaning in the world, to denote only its own meaning and thus to annul itself. We owe to poetic reflection some of the cardinal texts of modern Western poetry, poems in which our history is at once assumed and consumed:

negation of itself and of traditional meanings, an attempt to establish another meaning. Spaniards have seldom felt distrust before the word, seldom experienced that dizziness which consists of seeing language as the *sign of nothingness*. For Cernuda meditation—almost in the medical sense: to watch—consists of leaning on another mystery: that of our own passing. Life, not language. Between living and thinking, the word is not an abyss but a bridge. Meditation: mediation. The word expresses the distance between what I am and what I am being; at the same time, it is the only way of transcending that distance. By means of the word my life is arrested without pausing and sees itself seeing itself; by means of it I catch up with myself and pass myself by, and contemplate myself and turn into someone else—*another myself* who taunts my misery and in whose taunt my entire redemption is summarized.

The tension between a life ignorant of itself and conscience of self is resolved in the transparent word. Not in an impossible beyond, but here, in the instant of the poem, reality and desire reach an accord. And that embrace is so intense that it not only evokes the image of love but also that of death: in the breast of the poet, "just like a lute, death, death only, can make sound the promised melody." Few modern poets, in any language, give us this chilling sense of knowing ourselves to be before a man who *really speaks*, effectively possessed by the fatality and the lucidity of passion. If it were possible to define in a phrase the place Cernuda occupies in modern Spanish-language poetry, I would say he is the poet who speaks not for all, but for each one of us who make up the all. And he wounds us in the core of that part of each of us "which is not called glory, fortune, or ambition" but *the truth of ourselves*. For Cernuda the object of poetry was to know himself, but, with the same intensity, it was an attempt to create his own proper image. Poetic biography, *La realidad y el deseo* is something more, too: it is the history of a spirit which, in its self-recognition, transfigures itself.

III

It is now customary to say that Cernuda is a love poet. That is true, and from this theme all the others spring: solitude, boredom, exaltation of the natural world, contemplation of the works of men. . . . But one must begin by stressing something he never concealed: his love was homosexual and he did not know or speak of any other. There is no possible doubt: with admirable courage, if one considers the Spanish public and literary establishment, he wrote *boy* where others prefer to use more ambiguous nouns. "The truth of myself," he said in a poem he wrote in his youth, "is the truth of my actual love." His sincerity is not a taste for scandal nor a challenge to society (his challenge is elsewhere): it is an intellectual and moral point of honor. Moreover, one runs the risk of missing the point of his work if one omits or attenuates his homosexuality, not because his poetry can be reduced to that passion—that would be as wrong as to ignore it—but because it is the point of departure of his poetic creation. His erotic preferences do not explain his poetry, but without them his work would be different. His "different truth" sets him apart from the world at large; and that same truth, in a second movement, leads him on to discover a further truth, his and all of ours.

Gide gave him the courage to give things their proper names; the second book of his surrealist period is called *Los placeres prohibidos* (*Forbidden Pleasures*). He does not call them, as one might have expected, *perverse* pleasures. If one needs pluck to publish this kind of book in the 1930s in Spain, one needs still greater lucidity of mind to resist the temptation of adopting the role of ostracized rebel. The rebellion is ambiguous; those who affirm their "wickedness" consecrate the divine or social authority that condemns them; the condemnation includes them, negatively, in the order which they violate. Cernuda does not feel himself to be wicked: he feels excluded. And he doesn't lament this: he gives back blow for blow. The difference between him and a writer like Genet is revealing. Genet's challenge to the social world is more symbolic than real, and thus to make his gesture dangerous he has had to go further: eulogy of theft and treason, cult of criminals. Confronted by a society in which the honor of husbands still resides between the legs of women and in which "machismo" is a widespread disease, Cernuda's frankness exposed him to all sorts of actual risks, physical and moral. On the other hand, Genet is marked by Christianity—a negative Christianity; the sign of original sin is his homosexuality, or, more precisely, through it and in it is revealed the original stain: all of his deeds and works are the challenge and homage that nothingness raises against being. In Cernuda the sense of guilt hardly appears, and against Christian values he sets up others, his own, which seem to him the only true ones. It would be hard to find, in the Spanish language, a less Christian writer. Genet ends in the negation of negation: the black men who are white who are black who are white in his play. It is what Nietzsche called "incomplete nihilism," which does not transcend itself nor take itself for granted and is content to put up with itself. A Christianity without Christ. Cernuda's subversiveness is simpler, more radical, more sane.

To recognize one's homosexuality is to accept that one is different from others. But who are the others? The others are the world at large—and the world belongs to the others. In that world with the same fury heterosexual lovers, the revolutionary, the black, the proletarian, the expropriated bourgeois, the lone poet, the half-wit, the eccentric, and the saint are pursued. The others pursue everyone and no one. They are everyone and no one. Public health is the collective illness sanctified by force. Are the others real? A faceless majority or an all-powerful minority, they are a gaggle of ghosts. My body is real: is sin real? Prisons are real: are laws real as well? Between man and what he touches there is a zone of unreality: evil. The world is built on a negation, and institutions—religion, family, property, state, fatherland—are ferocious embodiments of that universal negation. To destroy this unreal world so that at last the true reality might emerge. . . . Any young person—not only a homosexual poet—can (and should) reflect on this. Cernuda accepts that he is different; modern thought, especially surrealism, shows him that we are all different. Homosexuality becomes synonymous with liberty; instinct is not a blind impulse: it is criticism transformed into deed. Everything, the body itself, acquires a *moral coloring*. In these years (1930) he becomes a Communist. A fleeting commitment, since in this matter as in so many others the Trojans are as stupid as the Greeks. The affirmation of his own truth makes him recognize the truth of others: "because of my pain I understand that others suffer greatly," he was to say years later. Though he shares our common destiny, he does not propose a panacea to us. He is a poet, not a reformer. He offers us his "true truth," that love which is the only liberty that exalts him, the only liberty worth dying for.

The true truth, his and everyone else's, is called desire. In a tradition which, with very few exceptions—they can be counted on the fingers, from *La celestina* and *La lozana andaluza* to Rubén Darío, Valle-Inclán, and García Lorca—identifies "pleasure" with "agreeable sensation, spiritual contentment, or diversion," Cernuda's poetry violently affirms the primacy of eroticism. That violence grows calmer with the years, but pleasure continues to occupy a central place in his work, beside its opposite-complement: solitude. They are the pair which govern his world, that "landscape of brooding ash" which desire peoples with radiant bodies, beautiful and glowing savages. From Baudelaire to Breton, the destiny of the word *desire* is confused with that of poetry. Its meaning is not psychological. Changing and still the same, it is energy, time's will to become embodied, vital hunger or anguish of death: it has no name and all names. What or who desires what we desire? Though it takes on the form of fate, it is not fulfilled without our liberty and in it one can read all our free will. We know nothing of desire, except that it crystallizes into images and that those images do not cease to trouble us until they become realities. We hardly touch them, and they disappear. Or is it we who disappear? Imagination is desire in motion. It is the imminent, what summons up the Apparition; and it is the distance which erases it. With a certain laziness one tends to see in Cernuda's poems mere variations on an old commonplace: reality in the end destroys desire, our life is a continual oscillation between privation and satiety. It seems to me that they say something else as well, something more true and terrible: if desire is real, reality is unreal. Desire makes the imaginary real, it makes reality unreal. The whole being of man is the theater of this continual metamorphosis; in his body and soul desire and reality interpenetrate and change, join and divide. Desire peoples the world with images and unpeoples reality at the same time. Nothing satisfies it because it turns living beings into ghosts. It feeds on shadows, or better said, our human reality, our substance, time and blood, nourish its shadows.

There is a point of intersection between desire and reality: love. Desire is vaster than love, but love-desire is the most powerful of desires. Only in that desiring of one being among all others does desire expand to its fullest extent. Who knows love wants nothing else. Love reveals reality to desire: that desired image is something more than a body which vanishes: it is a soul, a conscience. The erotic object turns into the beloved person. By means of love, desire at last touches reality: the other exists. This revelation is almost always painful because the existence of the other presents itself to us simultaneously as a body which is penetrable and a consciousness which is not. Love is the revelation of an alien liberty, and nothing is harder than to acknowledge the liberty of others, above all that of a person who is loved and desired. On this rests the contradiction of love: desire aspires to consummate itself by the destruction of the desired object; love discovers that that object is indestructible . . . and nothing can be put in its place. What is left is desire without love or love without desire. The first dooms us to solitude: those interchangeable bodies are unreal; the second is inhumane: can what is not desired be loved?

Cernuda was very aware of this genuinely tragic condition of love, of all love. In the poems of his youth the violence of his passion blindly collides with the unexpected existence of an irremediably alien conscience, and that discovery fills him with rage and shame. (Later, in a prose text, he alludes to the "egoism" of youthful loves.) In the books of his maturity the theme of Western love and mystical poetry—"the beloved transformed into the lover"—appears frequently. But union, the ultimate end of love, can be achieved only if it is realized that the other is a different and free being: if our love, instead of trying to abolish that difference, turns into the space in which it can unfold. Amorous union is not identity (if it were we would be more than men) but a state of perpetual mobility like play or, like music, of perpetual recapitulation. Cernuda always affirmed his different truth: did he see and acknowledge the truth of others? His work provides a double answer. Like almost all human beings—at least, like all those who really love, and there are not that many of them—in the moment of passion he is alternatively worshiper and adversary of his beloved; later, in the hour of reflection, he understands bitterly that if they did not love him as he wanted it was perhaps because he did not himself know how to love entirely disinterestedly. To love we ought to overcome ourselves, suppress the conflict between desire and love—without suppressing either one or the other. Difficult union between contemplative and active love. Not without struggles and vacillations did Cernuda aspire to this, the highest union; and that aspiration indicates the meaning of the evolution of his poetry: the violence of desire that never ceases to be desire tends to develop into the contemplation of a loved person. When I write that down, I am troubled by a doubt: can one speak of a loved person in Cernuda's case? I am thinking not only of the temper of homosexual love—with its underlying narcissism and its dependence on the world of childhood, which makes it capricious, tyrannical, and vulnerable to the illness of jealousy—but also of the disturbing insistence of the poet on considering love as an almost impersonal, fated thing.

In one poem from *Como quien espera el alba* (1947) he says: "Love and not the beloved is eternal." Fifteen or twenty years earlier he had said the same thing, with greater exasperation: "It is not love that dies, but we ourselves." In both instances he affirms the primacy of love over lovers, but in the poem of his youth he stresses man's death and love's immortality. The difference in tone shows the meaning of his spiritual evolution: in the second text love is no longer immortal but eternal and the "we" becomes "the beloved." The poet does not participate: he sees. He moves from active to contemplative love. What is remarkable is that this change does not alter the central vision: it is not men who realize themselves in love but love which makes use of men to realize itself. The idea of the human being as a "plaything of passion" is a constant theme in his poetry. Exaltation of love and a debasement of men. Our little value derives from our mortal condition: we are changed and we do not resist the changes of passion; we aspire to eternity and one instant of love destroys us. Deprived of its spiritual sustenance—the *soul* which Platonists and Christians gave him—the creature is not a person but a momentary condensation of inhuman powers: youth, beauty, and other magnetic forms in which time and energy manifest themselves. The creature is an apparition and there is nothing behind it. Cernuda seldom uses the words *soul* or *conscience* in speaking of his lovers; nor does he even allude to their particular physical characteristics, or to those attributes which, as the vulgar expression has it, give people "personality." In his world the face, mirror of the soul, does not reign, but the body. What this word means for the Spanish poet will not be understood unless it is stressed that in the human body he perceives the code of the universe. A young body is a solar system, a nucleus of physical and psychic irradiations. The body is the source of energy, a fountain of "psychic matter" or manna, a substance neither spiritual nor physical, a force which, according to primitive men, moves the world. When we love a body we do not adore a person but an embodiment of that cosmic force. Cernuda's love poetry goes from idolatry to veneration, from sadism to masochism; he suffers and delights with that will to preserve and to destroy the thing we love, in which consists the conflict between desire and love—but he ignores the otherness. It is a contemplation of *that which is loved*, not of the lover. Thus in the conscience of the other person he sees nothing but his own questioning face. That was his "true truth, the truth of himself." There is another truth; each time we love we lose ourselves: we are other, love does not realize the I myself: it opens up a possibility for the I to change and develop. In love it is not the I that is fulfilled but the person: the desire to be other. The desire to be.

If loving is desire, no law which is not the law of desire can subject it. For Cernuda love is a break with the social order and a joining with the natural world. And it is a break not only because his love differs from that of most but because all love shatters human laws. Homosexuality is not exceptional; the really exceptional thing is love. Cernuda's passion—and also his rage, his blasphemies and sarcasms—spring from a common root: from its origin Western poetry has never ceased to proclaim that the passion of love, the highest experience of our civilization, is a transgression, a social crime. The words of Melibea, the moment before she hurled herself from the tower, words of the fall and perdition but equally of blame for her father: all lovers can repeat them. Even in a society like that of the Hindus, which has not made love the chief passion, when the god Krishna puts on flesh and makes himself a man, he falls in love; and his loves are adulteries. It must be repeated again and again: love, all love, is immoral. Let us imagine a society different from ours and all those that history has known, a society in which the most complete erotic liberty prevailed, whether the infernal world of Sade or the paradisal world that modern sexologists propose to us: there love would be an even greater scandal than it is here among us. Natural passion, revelation of being in the person loved, bridge between this world and the next, contemplation of life or death: love opens the doors to a state which escapes the laws of common sense and current morality. No, Cernuda did not defend the right of homosexuals to live their life (that's a problem for social legislation) but he exalted as man's supreme experience the experience of love. A passion which takes on this or that form, always different and, nonetheless, always the same. Unique love for a unique person—though it is subject to change, disease, betrayal, and death. This was the only eternity he desired and the only truth he believed to be dependable. Not the truth of man: the truth of love.

In a world scoured by the criticism of reason and the wind of passion, so-called values become a scattering of ashes. What survives? Cernuda returns to ancient nature and discovers in it not God but the divinity herself, the mother of gods and myths. The power of love does not proceed from men, weak beings, but from the energy which moves all things. Nature is neither matter nor spirit for Cernuda: it is movement and form, it is appearance and it is invisible breath, word and silence. It is a language and more: a music. Its changes have no finality: it ignores morality, progress, and history; it is enough for it that it is, as is the case with God. And like God it cannot go beyond itself because it has no limits and all its transcendence is endlessly to contemplate and reflect itself, nature is a ceaseless changing of appearances and an always remaining the same as itself. An endless interplay, which means nothing and in which we can find no salvation or damnation at all. To watch it play with us, to play with it, to fall with and into it—that is our destiny. In this vision of the world there is more than a trace of *The Joyful Wisdom* and, above all, of the pessimism of Leopardi. World without creator though breathed over by a poetic breath, something I do not know whether or not to call religious atheism. True, at times God appears: he is the being with whom Cernuda talks when he talks with no one and who vanishes silently as a momentary cloud. He might be called an embodiment of nothing—and it returns to nothing. And yet veneration, in the sense of respect for the holy and divine, which skies and mountains, a tree, a bird, the sea, always the sea, inspire in him, are constant features from his first to his last book. He is a poet of love but also of the natural world. Its mystery fascinated him. He proceeds from a fusion with the elements to a contemplation of them, a development parallel to that of his love poetry. Sometimes his landscapes are arrested time and in them light thinks as it does in some of Turner's paintings; others are built up with the geometry of Poussin, a painter he was among the first to rediscover. Faced with nature, man does not cut a very good figure either: youth and beauty do not save him from his insignificance. Cernuda does not see in our unworthiness a trace of the fall, still less some proof of future salvation. The nothingness of man is without remission. He is a bubble of being.

Cernuda's negation resolves itself into an exaltation of realities and values which our world degrades. His destruction is creation, or better said, the resurrection of occult powers. Faced with traditional religion and morality and the substitutes which industrial society offers us, he affirms the contradictory pair desire-love; faced with the promiscuous solitude of cities, solitary nature. What is man's place? He is too weak to resist the tension between love and desire; nor is he a tree, cloud, or river. Between nature and passion, both inhuman, there is our consciousness. Our misery consists in our being time; a time which runs out. This lack is wealth: because we are finite time we are memory, understanding, will. Man remembers, knows, and works: he penetrates into the past, present, and future. In his hands time is a malleable substance; in converting it into the raw material of his deeds, thoughts, and works, man avenges himself on time.

There are three ways into time in Cernuda's poetry. The first is what is called an *accord*, the sudden discovery (by means of a landscape, a body, or music) of that paradox which is to *see* time hesitate without ceasing to flow: "timeless instant . . . fullness which, repeated through a lifetime, is always the same . . . what most resembles it is that getting inward by means of another body at the moment of ecstasy." Everyone, children and lovers, we have all felt something like this; what distinguishes the poet from others is the frequency and, most of all, the consciousness of those states and the need to express them. Another road, different from that of fusion with the instant, is that of contemplation. We look at any reality—a clump of trees, the shadow which brims a room at nightfall, a pile of rocks beside the road—we look without taking note, until slowly what we see reveals itself as the never seen and, at the same time, as the always seen: "looking, looking . . . nature likes to conceal itself and one must surprise it watching for long periods, passionately . . . looking and word make the poet." Do we look or do things look at us? And what we see, are they things or is it time which condenses itself into an appearance and then dissolves? In this experience distance intervenes; man does not become fused with externality, but his look creates between it and his conscience a space, propitious for revelation. What Pierre Schneider calls mediation. The third way is the vision of human works and of the work itself. After *Las nubes* it is one of his central themes and it is expressed mainly in two ways: the double (characters from myth, poetry, and history) and meditation on works of art. This is how he gains access to historical, human time.

In a note which precedes the selection of his poems in the *Antología* of Gerardo Diego (1930), Cernuda says that the only life which seems to him worth living is that of mythological or poetic beings, like the *Hyperion* of Hölderlin. This should not be taken as a challenge or an uncharacteristic statement; he always thought that daily reality suffers from unreality and that the true reality is that of imagination. What makes daily life unreal is the deceptive character of communication between people. Human communication is a fraud or, at least, an involuntary lie. In the world of the imagination things and beings are more of a piece and complete; the word does not conceal but reveals. In "Dístico español," one of his last poems, the real reality of Spain turns for him into an "obstinate nightmare: it is the land of the dead and in it everything is born dead"; he challenges that Spain with another, imaginary but more real, inhabited by "heroes loved in an heroic world," neither closed nor grudging but "tolerant of contrary loyalty, in accordance with the generous tradition of Cervantes." The Spain of Galdós's novels shows him that daily life is dramatic and that in the darkest existence "the paradox of being alive" is latent. Among those novel characters it is not strange that he should recognize himself in Salvador Monsalud, the "Frenchified" revolutionary and the fantastic lover, who never surrenders to the unreasonable mess that we call reality. And what young Latin American has not longed to be Salvador Monsalud: to fall in love with Genara and Adriana; to fight against the "ultras" and also against the "charlatan who deceives the people with his silvery spittle," to feel torn between horror and pity for the brother mad and in love with the same woman, the somnambulant Carlist guerrilla, the fratricide Carlos Garrote; who has not wished in the end to find *Soledad*, that reality more real and strong than all the passions?

Who does the poet address when he talks to a hero of myth or of literature? Each of us has in us a secret interlocutor. He is our double and something more: our contradictor, our confidante, our judge and only friend. The man who cannot talk alone to himself will be unable to talk truly with others. When he addresses myth creatures, Cernuda speaks for his own benefit, but in this way he talks to us. It is a dialogue which aims obliquely to elicit our response. The moment of reading is a now in which, as in a mirror, the dialogue between the poet and his imaginary visitor is reflected in the dialogue between the reader and the poet. The reader sees himself in Cernuda who sees himself in a phantom. Each seeks his own reality, his truth, in the imaginary character. Besides figures from myth and poetry, there are historical persons: Góngora, Larra, Tiberius. Rebels, marginalized beings, exiled by the stupidity of their contemporaries or by the fatal course of their own passions, are also masks, personae. Cernuda does not hide behind them; on the contrary, by means of them he recognizes and goes deeper into himself. The old literary device ceases to be that when it is changed into an exercise in introspection. In the poem dedicated to Ludwig of Bavaria, another of his last works, the king is alone in the theater and listens to the music "fused with the myth as he contemplates it: the melody helps him *to know himself, to fall in love with what he himself is*." In speaking of the king, Cernuda writes of but not for himself; he invites us to contemplate his myth and to repeat his gesture: self-knowledge through the alien object.

Faced with the Escorial palace, or a Titian canvas or Mozart's music, he perceives a truth vaster than his own, though it is not contradictory or excluding. In works of art time makes use of men to fulfill itself. But it is time made solid, humanized: an epoch. Fusion with the moment or contemplation of ephemerality are experiences in and of time, but in a certain sense outside history; the vision which a work of art provides is an experience of historical time. On the one hand, the work is what is commonly called an expression of history, dated time; on the other, it is an archetype of what a man can do with his time: turn it into stone, music, or language, transmute it in form, and infuse it with meaning. Open it out to the understanding of others: return it to the present. The vision of the work implies dialogue, recognition of a truth distinct from ours and which, nonetheless, directly con-

217

cerns us. The work of art is a presence from the past made continually present. However incomplete and poor our experience, we repeat the creator's gesture and we go through the process in the opposite direction to the artist's; we move from a contemplation of the work to an understanding of its occasion: a situation, a concrete time. Dialogue with works of art consists not only of hearing what they say but of re-creating, reliving them as presences: to awaken their present. It is a creative repetition. In Cernuda's case the experience serves him, moreover, to understand his mission as a poet better. The initial rupture with the social order is followed by participation in history—but without betraying the rebellious stance which, in substance, remained the same until his death. Thus the creations of others bring him to a consciousness of his task: history is not only time lived and died but time which is transmuted into work and deed.

In contemplating this or that creation, Cernuda perceives that fusion between the individual will of the artist and the will, almost always unconscious, of his time and world. He discovers that he writes not only to tell the "truth about himself"; his true truth is also that of his language and his people. The poet gives a voice "to the mute mouths of his own kind" and thus frees them. The "others" have become "his own." But to state that truth it is not a matter of repeating the commonplaces of the pulpit, the public tribunal, the council of ministers, or the radio. The truth of all is not at variance with the conscience of the solitary nor is it less subversive than individual truth. This truth, which cannot be confused with majority or minority opinions, is concealed, and it is the poet's job to reveal it, free it. The cycle opened in the poems of his youth closes: negation of the world which we call real and affirmation that the reality that is real is the one that desire and creative imagination reveal; exaltation of natural powers and recognition of man's task on earth: to create works, to make life out of dead time, to give meaning to blind transience; rejection of a false tradition and discovery of a history which has not ended yet and into which his life and his work are woven as if in new accord. At the end of his days, Cernuda is unsure whether to credit the reality of his work or the unreality of his life. His book was his real life and was constructed hour by hour, as one might raise a building. He built with living time and his word was *scandalstone*. He has left us a body of work which is in every sense *edifying*.

Delhi, 24 May 1964